The Saltoun Papers

Reflections on Andrew Fletcher

Edited by
Paul Henderson Scott

THE
SALTIRE SOCIETY

The Saltoun Papers published 2003 by

The Saltire Society
9 Fountain Close,
22 High Street,
Edinburgh EH1 1TF

A catalogue record for this book is available
from the British Library.

ISBN 0 85411 081 X

The publisher is very grateful to the Scottish Arts Council
for financial assistance in the publication of this book

Cover design by James Hutcheson

Printed and bound in Scotland by Bell and Bain Limited

THE SALTOUN PAPERS
refelections on andrew fletcher of saltoun

CONTENTS

Introduction

Since the 1960s Andrew Fletcher of Saltoun has been commemorated each September with a speech about him in the kirk of East Saltoun, where he is buried. As David Simpson recalls in his contribution to this book, this practice was established by David Mill Irving, a retired British Ambassador and President of the Haddington Branch of the SNP. Wendy Wood and Nigel Tranter were among those who spoke in this period. Since the 1970s the Saltire Society has carried on this tradition, originally under the direction of A. C. Davies and then for many years of Robin MacCormick.

This book contains a selection of the papers which have been delivered in the last twenty years. Unfortunately, I have not been able to recover all of the texts. David Daiches, Donny O'Rourke and Alex Salmond all spoke brilliantly without notes. Michael Lynch is the victim of a computer which refuses to divulge much of the work entrusted to it. Among other points, he spoke about the pre-Union Scottish Parliament and the volume of enlightened and sensible legislation which it produced.

The papers which we now reprint are diverse in their approach and together cover a wide range of Scottish history and ideas. Bruce Lenman takes the continuing relevance of Fletcher as his theme and William Ferguson remarks that there is a timeless quality about him. This collection of papers is a convincing demonstration that they are right. Fletcher naturally stimulates thought on political and constitutional questions and on the nature of patriotism and nationalism; but Arnold Kemp, Billy Kay and Sheila Douglas find his ideas relevant to other aspects of contemporary life. There are significant points of agreement between several of the papers. Billy Kay, for instance, deplores the effect of mass communications, especially television, on Scottish culture. Geoffrey Barrow considers that the failure to establish a national Scottish organisation for radio and television (a failure continued in the reserved powers imposed on the Scottish Parliament) to be "surely the most astonishing single feature in the collective life or twentieth-century Scotland". Gordon Donaldson notes the resemblance of Fletcher's thought to the ideas in the Declaration of Arbroath and Edward Cowan his indebtedness to a distinctive Scottish tradition in radical political thinking.

The papers are printed in the chronological order in which they were given. References in them to the situation at the time reflect the changing political circumstances.

One or two of the papers suggest that Fletcher was an advocate of federalism. As far as the surviving evidence goes, there are no grounds for this idea. Some confusion has derived from his references in two documents to 'uniting'. In a letter which he wrote in 1689, and to which T. C. Smout has drawn attention, Fletcher spoke about 'uniting with England in Parliaments and trade', but not 'in worship and particular laws'. Also in his pamphlet *An Account of a Conversation* immediately after arguing robustly for Scottish independence and European co-operation, he again refers to the need to be 'united with England'. There is nothing inconsistent about these remarks if we take account of the meaning of the word union and its derivatives at the time when Fletcher was writing.

The historical examples in the *Oxford Dictionary* show that the usual meaning of the word before it acquired a special sense in 1707 was agreement or association of any kind or merely the absence of dissension or discord. It did not imply a constitutional arrangement of any kind, federal or other.

There is, of course, a variety of political attitudes in these papers. David Simpson represents the views of the SNP and John Home Robertson MSP of the Labour Party. Iain Noble considers the constitutional options from a business point of view. In his paper Robertson asks if Scotland would be content to be another Denmark or Ireland (presumably meaning the Republic and not the North). He seems to expect us to have some nostalgia for the long gone days of Empire. In fact, the status of Denmark or Ireland is precisely what many of us would like. A comparison by any standard of measurement between Scotland and our European neighbours who have retained, or regained, independence shows, I think, how right Fletcher was to defend our independence and warn against 'the miserable and languishing condition of all places that depend upon a remote seat of government'. John Home Robertson is right to say that 'we have a well developed awareness of international affairs and we expect to be involved'. It is precisely for that reason, as again Fletcher would agree, that Scotland needs the status that would make involvement possible.

P.H.S.
Edinburgh
January 2003

Books for Further Reading

There are two modern editions of Fletcher's works: *Fletcher of Saltoun, Selected Writings*, edited by David Daiches (Scottish Academic Press for the Association for Scottish Literary Studies, Edinburgh, 1970) and Andrew Fletcher, *Political Works*, edited by J.Robertson (Cambridge University Press, 1997).

The best contemporary account of Fletcher is to be found in the vivid memoirs of one of his supporters in the Scottish Parliament, George Lockhart of Carnwath. There is a recent edition: *"Scotland's Ruine"; Lockhart of Carnwath's Memoirs of the Union*, edited by Daniel Szechi with a Foreword by Paul Scott. (The Association for Scottish Literary Studies, Aberdeen, 1995)

There are three Saltire Society publications which are very relevant: William Ferguson's *Scotland's Relations with England - A Survey to 1707* (Edinburgh, 1977 and 1994) and my *Andrew Fletcher and the Treaty of Union* (Edinburgh, 1992 and 1994) and *The Boasted Advantages: The Consequences of the Union of 1707* (Edinburgh, 1909).

P. S

Other Books by Paul Henderson Scott

1707: The Union of Scotland and England Chambers 1979
Walter Scott and Scotland Saltire Society 1994
John Galt Scottish Academic Press 1985
In Bed with an Elephant Saltire Society 1985
The Thinking Notion University of Dundee 1989
Towards Independence: Essays on Scotland Polygon 1991 and 1996
Andrew Fletcher and the Treaty of Union Saltire Society 1994
Scotland in Europe: A Dialogue with a Sceptical Friend Canongate 1992
Defoe in Edinburgh and Other Papers Tuckwell Press 1995
A Mad God's Dream Edinburgh District Council 1997
Still in Bed with an Elephant Saltire Society 1998
The Boasted Advantages Saltire Society 1999
A Twentieth Century Life Argyll Publishing 2002

edited

The Age of MacDiarmid Mainstream 1980 (with AC Davis)
Sir Walter Scott's The Letters of Malachi Malagrowther Blackwoods 1981
Andrew Fletcher's United and Separate Parliaments Saltire Society 1982
A Scottish Postbag Saltire Society 2002 (with George Bruce)
Scotland: A Concise Cultural History Mainstream 1993
Scotland's Ruine: Lockhart of Carnwath's Memoirs of the Union Association for Scottish Literary Studies 1995 (with Daniel Szechi)
John Galt's The Member and The Radical Canongate 1996 (with Ian Gordon)
Scotland: An Unwon Cause Canongate 1997

1979

Fletcher of Saltoun

Gordon Donaldson

Gordon Donaldson (1913-1993) was Professor of Scottish History at Edinburgh University from 1963 until 1979 when he was appointed Historiographer Royal. His publications include: *Scotland: James V to James VII* (volume 3 of the Edinburgh history of Scotland, 1965). *Scottish Kings* (1967). *Who's who in Scottish History* (1913), *The Auld Alliance* (1985), *Scotland's History: Approaches and Reflection* (edited by James Kirk 1995).

Fletcher of Saltoun

Gordon Donaldson

This assignment to speak here today to honour the memory of Fletcher of Saltoun recalls to my mind two earlier assignments I have had. Five years ago, in 1974, which was the seventh centenary of the birth of Robert Bruce, I was asked by the National Trust to give what they were pleased to call an oration on the Field of Bannockburn on 24th June. And ten years ago, in 1969, I gave an address in St Mary's Cathedral, Edinburgh, in honour of the memory of King Charles I, on 30 January, the anniversary of his beheading.

When I spoke about Charles I, I remarked, as I have often done, that historians like to be on the winning side and that history is on the whole written on the assumption that what happened in the end was for the best. Few people seem to like admitting that things may from time to time have gone wrong. Consequently, the failures in history, those who have been on the losing side, usually get a bad press.

Now Fletcher, I suppose, was a failure, to the extent that the cause he supported turned out to be the losing cause, and it would commonly be said that he miscalculated. He certainly seems to have been convinced that the union would <u>not</u> pass and that he would be on the winning side. But even had he been sure it <u>would</u> pass he would still have had the courage of his convictions and opposed it. There had been a similar incident in his earlier life. When Monmouth was planning his rebellion against James VII and II, Fletcher said it was folly to think of trying to conquer England by landing only a small force and not ensuring in advance the support of a body of the nobility. Yet when the time came, he took his stand with Monmouth, out of a purely chivalrous attachment to him. At that stage he was rather like Lord George Murray in the '45, for Lord George entered on that rising although he had little hope it would succeed, and said: 'My life, my fortune, my expectations, the happiness of my wife and children are all at stake (and the chances are against me) and yet a principle of what seems to me honour and duty to my king and country outweighs everything'. There was a certain nobility about that kind of Jacobitism, and there was a certain nobility about Fletcher too. Fletcher was not afraid to be a failure, an honourable failure.

And yet, unlike most failures, Fletcher has not had a bad press. He is an exception to the rule. For this I think there are two reasons. One is the qualities of the man himself, his lack of selfishness and his single-mindedness. A Whig contemporary assessed him thus: 'He would lose his life readily to serve his country and would not do a base thing to save it'. And a Jacobite was no less favourable: 'He never once pursued a measure with the prospect of any by end to himself, no further than he judges it for the common benefit and advantage of his country'.

The second reason why Fletcher, unlike most failures, has had a good press is perhaps equally obvious. It is that the debate in which he was involved has never been closed, but continues. And when I say that I do not mean — though this is true too — that the advantages and disadvantages of Anglo-Scottish union are still being discussed today. What I mean is that historians are still discussing the reasons why union did come about in 1707.

This is a topic which must often recur to the mind of a Scottish historian, and it has been peculiarly fresh in my mind in recent weeks, as a result of reading Dr Riley's recent books on King William's reign and the Union. It's quite extraordinary how fashions in historical interpretation change, and anyone who has been in the business as long as I have has learned not to be 'tossed to and fro, carried about by every wind of doctrine', as if the latest theory is necessarily the last word on the subject. The cynic might say that historical judgment goes round in circles.

It was long the conventional view that the constitutional change at the Revolution, resulting in two independent parliaments under a single monarch, produced an unstable situation which could be resolved only by either the complete separation of England and Scotland or the union of the two parliaments, and that 1707 was thus the inevitable consequence of 1688-9. This interpretation has been challenged in the last generation, but Dr Riley has reverted to it. He says: 'Failing a union of the two kingdoms, the task of governing Scotland was an impossible one . . .The revolution settlement and William's misunderstanding of the situation it created had made union necessary'. He makes it clear that the proceedings of the Scottish parliament in 1703-4 — proceedings in which Fletcher played a prominent part — were effective as bargaining counters, with the result that the Scots were able to demand far more, and the English ready to concede far more, in 1706-7 than they had been in the abortive negotiations of 1702-3. In the end, Dr Riley suggests, the Scots 'could hardly have gained more'. On this interpretation, you see, rather paradoxically and ironically, Fletcher's activities did play their part in shaping the treaty of union and gaining concessions for his country. Thanks to Fletcher, it was a better treaty, from the Scottish point of view, than it might have been.

Dr Riley can see that there were sound arguments both for and against the union, but his greatest merit is that, unlike most critics of the union, he courageously faces the fact that the alternative to union was the armed conquest of Scotland by England. Union was 'the only feasible solution', because 'the English would not tolerate an independent Scotland'. Failing union, there was 'no future but anarchy, civil war and English conquest', so that, Riley concludes, 'those who condemn what happened in 1707. . . should reflect on the dire alternative . . . and say whether they find it acceptable'.

Whether Fletcher himself really faced that dire alternative it is hard to say; but it is even harder to believe that, faced with the choice, he would have preferred to see his country conquered by war rather than incorporated in a peaceful union. And — and this is too often forgotten — once union was an accomplished fact Fletcher was prepared to accept it. He did in fact stand for the constituency of East Lothian in the elections for the united parliament, but was defeated. One wonders what he would have made of the Westminster parliament. He had expressed the view that the Scottish MP's would be powerless: 'Their 15 Scots members may dance round to all Eternity, in this trap of their own making'. He did not foresee the development of the party system, which has brought it about that the Scottish voters have again and again determined the complexion of the British government.

There may even be a third reason why Fletcher, though a failure, gets a good press, in addition to his manifest integrity and the fact that the debates in which he engaged are still going on. This is the fact that he was of lairdly and not of noble stock. A parallel can easily be drawn between Fletcher of Saltoun and Wallace of Elderslie, the one a simple Renfrewshire country gentleman and the other a simple East Lothian country gentleman. The parallel is attractive to those who like to contrast the patriotism of the lairds with the supposed lack of patriotism of the nobles. This, I may say, is an over-simplified and even erroneous view.

The suspicions which have been circulated about the nobles have naturally added to the credit of country gentlemen like Fletcher, and the lairds are seen as the persistent repositories of the patriotic tradition. But look back for a moment at the Declaration of Arbroath, and recall the names of the men who put their names to that Declaration of Scottish Independence. Who were they? There is a long list of earls and lords, mostly of Norman extraction, and so aristocratic is the flavour of the whole thing that it is with something of a shock that near the end we suddenly come on the names of native lairds like Donald Campbell and Fergus of Ardrossan. Patriotic lairds were not conspicuous in 1320. That should be kept in mind as a kind of corrective to attempts to simplify the social pattern into which Fletcher fits.

And indeed there is a converse, I mean to the supposed lack of patriotism of the nobles. In the sixteenth century, in the era of Henry

VIII, the East Lothian lairds had been the best and most faithful friends England had had — far more reliable than the nobles. They turn up consistently protestant and anglophile in the 1540s, 1550s and 1560s.

However, to say that Fletcher, in opposing a union with England, was out of character as an East Lothian laird or was not in the tradition of East Lothian lairds, is nothing more than a debating point, for two reasons. In the first place, the Fletchers had not been very long in Saltoun. Indeed it was only in 1643, just in the previous generation, that a Fletcher had acquired the estate.

The other reason why we cannot think of Fletcher in the same way as earlier East Lothian lairds is that he was acting as a politician in completely novel circumstances. The Revolution which replaced James VII by William of Orange produced a completely new constitutional situation in Scotland. The parliament had asserted itself by dismissing one king and appointing another on terms tantamount to a contract. Then, in the new reign, some of the devices by which kings had formerly controlled parliament passed out of existence, and parliament could use the power of the purse as never before. But the parliament which thus gained in power was ill equipped for its new role. It is true that serious parliamentary opposition (in which Fletcher was involved) had emerged in Charles II's reign. But, although there were factions in plenty, there were not yet, even in William's reign, recognisable parties, like the English Whigs and Tories. Therefore, although politicians were groping towards the concept of a homogeneous administration (or opposition) of like-minded men, there were no parties on which to base such an administration (or opposition). Besides, the Scottish ministry had to seek the confidence not only of parliament, but also of the king, who still possessed considerable powers, and, because of the personal union, the complexion of a Scottish ministry could not in practice be detached from that of the English ministers who advised William as king of England. It was all very difficult, and the position would have tried the most expert statesmanship. Fletcher and his contemporaries were operating in a kind of quagmire, or in a fog, with few landmarks to guide them. They were feeling their way and were unsure of themselves. The existing machinery and the way it worked hardly matched their aims and intentions.

I said at the outset that this occasion recalled two previous occasions — an address in commemoration of Charles I and an address in commemoration of Robert Bruce. When I was preparing the oration in commemoration of Bruce, one of the thoughts that came into my mind — and it is a thought to which I have since given expression more than once both in print and in lectures — was this. In Bruce's period it was impossible to fight for Scotland without fighting also for a claimant to the throne. It was impossible to be as it were simply a patriot, impossible to be a patriot without being also the partisan of some dynasty, whether Bruce, Balliol or Comyn.

I do think a change occurred before the end of Bruce's life, and it is in this that I see particularly the significance of the Declaration of Arbroath in 1320. The point it professes to make is precisely that it is possible to dissociate patriotism from the support of a dynasty, possible to disentangle the national cause from a dynastic cause or the support of one claimant to the throne or another. To that extent unquestionably the most significant clause in the Declaration is of course the clause in which the barons declared that should Bruce show signs of giving up the struggle they would eject him and make another king, because, as they say, they are fighting not for him but for their liberty. It seems to me that that clause represents a great step forward in the evolution of the national outlook, and perhaps in the evolution of constitutional theory.

Now I believe that in Fletcher of Saltoun we see the continuation or perhaps the revival of that idea. In Fletcher we have a patriot who was emphatically not a dynast, not the supporter of a claimant to the throne, indeed rather careless as to who the king should be. He is sometimes said to have been a republican, but I don't think that is altogether true. Republicanism has been rare in Scotland, and apart from a few fringe politicians — not all of them in recent times — the only Scot of note I think of who was a republican was Andrew Carnegie, and of course he had ceased to be a Scot when he became an American. You remember what Carnegie replied when he was asked to subscribe to a memorial to King Robert Bruce?

> I hate with a bitter hatred and resent as an insult to my manhood the monarchical idea. A king is an insult to every other man in the land. Perish kings and queens and privilege in all its forms. If you have a man of the people who is thought worthy of a monument or of assistance and you obtain subscriptions for this man, I'll send you my £30, but not a penny for all the kings and queens in Christendom.

I do not think for a moment that Fletcher would have written in such terms. He might have been happy with a republic if Scotland had been a republic, but he could be equally happy with a king — on terms, not in virtue of inviolable descent. Curiously enough, Fletcher was himself half a Bruce, for his mother was Catherine Bruce, daughter of Sir Henry Bruce of Clackmannan, a family which claimed descent — though it was never precisely defined or proved — from the Bruces of Annandale, the family from which King Robert sprang. But I doubt if Fletcher would have attached much importance to that distant aristocratic or royal connection.

Fletcher, I suggest, would have been much more proud of the resemblance of his thought to that of the Declaration of Arbroath. The Declaration made it clear that King Robert had been raised to the throne not only by his right of succession but also by the due and lawful consent of all the people. The earlier Declaration, by the clergy in 1310, ten years earlier, had been even more emphatic that Robert had, with the concurrence and assent of the people, been chosen to be king and had, by the authority of the people, been set over the kingdom and made king. Now Fletcher had no regard for indefeasible hereditary succession and was opposed to prerogative powers in a king, but he did not press for elective monarchy either. It was to be hereditary with qualifications, we might almost say, hereditary unless . . . Now this was very much what the Declaration of Arbroath had said. Just as the barons who put their seals to that document declared that they would support Bruce as long as he supported the national cause, so I think Fletcher would have said he would support a king as long as the king supported the national cause but would give up the king, if the king gave up that cause.

But remember that the barons had emphasised that they were not fighting for a king, they were fighting for liberty. So it was with Fletcher. In his view either Stewart or Hanover would serve, provided his own famous limitations on monarchy were accepted — limitations which among other things excluded the royal veto on legislation, which gave parliament the control of peace or war and forbade an army without parliament's consent. The monarchy, Fletcher thought, should be limited or constitutional, it should be responsible to parliament. Given this, he did not care who sat on the throne, 'If we may live free, I little value who is king'. Is this not almost a paraphrase of the Declaration of Arbroath? 'If we may live free, I little value who is king', from Fletcher, and, from the Declaration, 'It is not for riches or honours or glory that we fight, but for liberty alone'. I see a remarkable consensus between the barons of 1320 and the East Lothian laird of 1707.

1984

Andrew Fletcher ,
a Pioneer of the European Idea

Paul Henderson Scott

Paul H Scott served in Diplomatic Service from 1950 to 1980. He was Vice-President of the Scottish National Party between 1991 and 97 and President, of The Saltire Society from 1996 until 2002. His publications include: *1707: The Union of Scotland and England* (1979): *Walter Scott and Scotland* (1981 and 1994), *John Galt* (1985); *Andrew Fletcher and the Treaty of Union* (1992 and 1994); *Defoe in Edinburgh* (1995); *Still in Bed with an Elephant* (1998); *Scotland: An Unwon Cause* (1997); *The Boasted Advantages* (1999); *A Twentieth Century Life* (2002).

Andrew Fletcher,
a Pioneer of the European Idea

Paul Henderson Scott

Andrew Fletcher of Saltoun, who lived from 1653 to 1716, has long had a remarkable reputation in Scotland. In this century he has acquired two additional reputations.

He is the only man in Scottish history who has been known quite simply as 'the Patriot', a distinction not accorded even to Wallace or Bruce. It was applied to Fletcher, almost from his own life-time, because of his determined and incorruptible resistance to the parliamentary Union of 1707. It was a time from which, as the historian Hume Brown said, we have tended 'by an unconscious instinct to avert our eyes'. English historians have been disinclined to linger over the spectacle of their countrymen acting the bully and applying bribery and military threats to their smaller neighbour. The Scots have had even less stomach to admit that their own parliamentarians accepted the bribes and yielded to the pressure. Against this background Fletcher was so striking an exception that he was admired by political friend and opponent alike.

This admiration has continued. David Hume said that he was 'a man of signal probity and fine genius' and Sir Walter Scott that he was 'one of the most accomplished men and best patriots, whom Scotland has produced in any age'. To this day Fletcher has been described in similar terms by a whole succession of speakers at this annual ceremony, here in the Kirk of East Saltoun, where he is buried.

In this century Fletcher has been rediscovered by political scientists, mainly American, who have been struck by the lucidity and originality of Fletcher's writings and by his contribution to the development of political thought. This is all contained in one book, *The Political Works*, published after his death, which reprinted five short pamphlets and a number of his speeches to the 1703 session of the Scottish Parliament. There were three further editions in the 18th century, but no other until David Daiches edited one for the Association of Scottish Literary Studies in 1979.

The Political Works make a slender volume, 136 pages in the Daiches edition, which may seem a frail foundation for the second reputation which Fletcher has achieved. Other works have been attributed to him, although few that can be accepted with much confidence. When I edited *State of the controversy Betwixt United and Separate Parliaments* for the Saltire Society in 1982, I said that I thought we should accept it as Fletcher's on the strong authority of his nephew and of Thomas Rudiman, a great scholar who was a contemporary of Fletcher's and the Librarian of the Advocates' Library. It certainly has some brilliant phrases, 'flashes as quick as lightening', as Sir John Dalrymple called them, which sound like Fletcher. But there are also some other remarks, including sycophantic references to the Queen, which I am sure Fletcher could never have brought himself to utter. So even this pamphlet, I now think, could at best be a collaborative effort in which Fletcher played a part.

One of the distinguishing features of Fletcher's writing, and it is a large part of the explanation why so few pages have been so influential, is its economy. There is no padding and hardly a wasted word. Very often he stated an idea, which may be significant and original, in a sentence or two or even a phrase. There is often more substance in a page of Fletcher's writing than in whole volumes by more laborious but less original thinkers. He writes in an easy, fluent idiomatic English, remarkable in a Scotsman of his time, when everyone outside the Highland line spoke Scots and educated men were more familiar with written Latin than spoken English. He anticipates, or you might say initiates, the Scottish Enlightenment in his analyses of the historical process. He recognises the importance of economic factors in a way which anticipates David Hume, Adam Smith and ultimately Karl Marx. He is an early advocate of the transfer of all power from the Monarch to Parliament and of the need for society to take responsibility for the workers in sickness and old age and for the education of their children.

The latest and very topical strand in Fletcher's reputation is his advocacy of the European idea. He was very much the European Scot. For two periods he was a political exile on the Continent, first because he had resisted the tyrannical regime of Lauderdale and secondly because of his involvement in Monmouth's rising. He seems to have fought in the Hungarian army against the Turks and he certainly acquired a reputation as an accomplished cavalry officer. Throughout his life he built up a great library, said to be the best in private hands in Scotland, which systematically included books on every country in Europe. He wrote a pamphlet in Italian to oppose the domination of Europe by a combination of the royal houses of Spain and France.

This pamphlet, *A Discourse concerning the Affairs of Spain*, was written, according to its title page, in July 1698. It was not included in the Daiches edition for the reasons, I suppose, that it stands outside the main body of Fletcher's work and is concerned with different subjects. It stood outside most obviously because it was written in Italian and purported to be published in Naples, although with the same paper and type as the other pamphlets published in Edinburgh. Why this mystification? The essay dealt with the European-wide problem of the consequences that were likely to follow from the imminent death of Charles II, King of Spain, who had no issue and no undisputed successor. There was a risk that the vast territories of the Spanish Empire might fall into the hands of the King of France and so create an immense power that could dominate the world. The Italian states were pawns in any possible settlement. Fletcher may therefore have felt that the pamphlet would have more influence if it appeared to come from an Italian source. John Robertson has suggested that Fletcher was reacting to a book, of which he had a copy in his library, *De Monarchia*

Hispanica by Tommaso Campanella. This was a plea for a universal empire under the King of Spain, which was precisely what Fletcher was anxious to oppose.

He went about this task in a spirit of Swiftian irony, a technique which is open to misunderstanding. In his essay Fletcher discused the various ways in which the succession to Charles II could lead to a world empire. The unwary reader might easily suppose that he was advocating it. Fletcher seems to have realised this after the publication of the first edition, because he added an explanatory note, or 'advertisement' in the language of the day, to the subsequent English translation. In this he said that he had written the essay about the risk of 'progress towards the empire of the world':

> not with a view of favouring the establishment of a government so hurtful to good manners, and so destructive of the general happiness of mankind, as a universal one is, and as all, great ones, whether republics or monarchies, in which power and riches are grown to an excessive height, cannot fail, to be.

This distrust of large and powerful governments is the fundamental core of Fletcher's political thought. It is developed in the most elaborate of his pamphlets, *An Account of a Conversation Concerning a Right Regulation of Governments for the Common Good of Mankind,* which purports to be a letter from London on the 1st of December, 1703. I say 'purports' because the conversation, which it describes, was probably largely imaginary, although it may have been based on one which actually took place. The participants were all real people, two members of the Scottish, and two of the English, Parliaments. Apart from Fletcher himself, the other Scot was the Earl of Cromartie, one of the very few people in Scotland who from the beginning was enthusiastically in favour of an incorporating Union. Of the two Englishmen, Sir Christopher Musgrave was a high Tory of solid reputation and the leader of his party. The other, Sir Edward Seymour, was also a prominent House of Commons man who had been speaker during the reign of Charles II. He was virulently anti-Scottish. In the dialogue Fletcher attributes to him a remark which he did in fact make in the Commons: 'What a pother is here about a union with Scotland, of which all the advantage we shall have, will be no more than what a man gets by marrying a beggar, a louse for her portion?'

The conversation begins with some preliminary pleasantries about London. It soon turns to constitutional matters when Seymour arrives and immediately launches an attack on Fletcher over his proposals for 'limitations'. Cromartie suggests an incorporating Union, although this had not so far been proposed in either Parliament. Fletcher vigorously defends Scotland's independence against any proposal to reduce it to what he calls, 'the miserable and languishing condition of all places that depend upon a remote seat of government'. Fletcher argues that the transfer of the royal prerogatives to London by the Union of the Crowns in 1603 had led to the reglect of Scotland, 'like a farm managed by servants and not under the eye of the master ... Since that time we have had neither spirit, nor liberty, nor trade, nor money among us'. He denies that an 'incorporating' union would have trading benefits for Scotland. He cites the example of Wales which after three or four hundred years of union 'has no considerable commerce, though possessed of one of the best ports in the whole island; a sufficient demonstration that trade is not a necessary consequence of a union with England'.

In the course of this discussion, Fletcher said that he was opposed to 'great and overgrown powers' which tended to corruption and which caused wars and great effusion of blood, both in their expansion and in their eventual overthrow and destruction. He is challenged by Musgrave to say what he thought would be a right division of territory into several distinct governments (he said of the world, but in practice the discussion is confined to Europe). This brings Fletcher to suggest that Europe falls naturally because of geography and climate, into seventeen 'provinces', or groups of countries. Each of these would be subdivided in turn into ten or twelve subdivisions, or sovereign cities as he calls them. They would be united on terms of equality for their common defence and none would be strong enough to attempt the conquest of any of the others.

It is typical of Fletcher that he throws out succinct hints like this of new and far-reaching ideas without attempting to develop them in any detail. His suggestion of a European system of small, autonomous but interlocking states is only a vague sketch, but it is recognisably a Europe of the regions.

Such an arrangement was, no doubt, visionary and Utopian at the time when Fletcher proposed it and there was no possibility that it could then be achieved. As Neal Ascherson has remarked, it is so no longer. The break-up of the empires and the multi-national states on the one hand, and the movement towards closer co-operation on the other, is now creating a Europe which begins to meet the ideals which Fletcher expressed in 1704.

After making the case for European co-operation, Fletcher in the same essay discussed the advantages of the dispersion of power. For him, as for E F. Schumacher, small is beautiful. He was opposed to large states and large towns which drew excessive power and wealth to themselves. London, which in many ways he admired, was such a case. 'This vast city is like the head of a rickety child' which draws to itself 'the nourishment that should be distibuted in due proportions to the rest of the languishing body . . . That London should draw the riches and government of the three kingdoms to the south-east corner of this island is in some degree as unnatural as for one city to possess the riches and government of the world'. All governments which imposed their will over distant peoples were 'violent, unjust and unnatural'. On the other hand, a diversity of small governments gave many men the opportunity of doing good to their fellow citizens and 'many different seats of government will highly tend to the improvement of all arts and sciences', as in the cities of ancient Greece. Later in the century David Hume repeated the same point.

Fletcher's vision for Scotland and for Europe were in accordance. He saw no inconsistency between his struggle to maintain and extend the independence of Scotland and his advocacy of an all-embracing European system. On the contrary it was the growth of large and multi-national states, such as the absorption of Scotland in an incorporating Union, which he saw as the denial of justice and good government and a threat to peace. The relevance of Fletcher's ideas to our current concerns both in Scotland and in Europe is inescapable. Scotland has been closely involved in the rest of Europe for many centuries. Andrew Fletcher of Saltoun was a great Scottish patriot, all the more so because he was also actively, learnedly and consciously European.

1985

Andrew Fletcher; a Sturdy Example

Geoffrey Barrow

Geoffrey W S Barrow was Professor of Scottish History at St Andrews University from 1974 to 79 and thereafter at the University of Edinburgh until 1992. He was President of the Saltire Society between 1987 and 1990. His publications include: *Robert Bruce and the Community of the Realm of Scotland* (1965-1988), *The Kingdom of the Scots* (1973), *Robert Bruce and the Scottish Identity* (1984)

Andrew Fletcher: a sturdy example

Geoffrey Barrow

Lord Hailes wrote in his *Annals of Scotland* of Thomas Randolph first earl of Moray, 'A man he was to be remembered while integrity, prudence and valour, are held in esteem among men,' I am not sure whether Randolph is now commemorated anywhere. In medieval times and for all I know, still in catholic countries and among catholic communities, perpetual commemoration could be and may yet be secured by the institution of a Requiem Mass. If Hailes's judgement was sound, as I believe it was, then Randolph was certainly worthy to be remembered, and if there were to be a formal commemoration ceremony I can think of no more fitting place for it than the simple parish kirk of Alvie in Badenoch, looking out over Loch Alvie and the Monadhliath. It was out of the surplus income from this little highland kirk that Randolph carefully provided for perpetual requiems to be celebrated in Elgin cathedral for his uncle, the hero king Robert I, and for himself and his family, an arrangement as carefully confirmed by John Pilmuir bishop of Moray and his former master Pope Clement VI.

With protestants, however, as of course with agnostics, atheists and countless others not of the Christian faith, commemoration cannot be fitted so easily into the daily or weekly round. That Fletcher of Saltoun had a character and career which fit him for commemoration admits of no doubt, although it has to be said that, of the qualities listed by Hailes, valour and integrity can be granted unreservedly, while prudence did not come naturally to Fletcher and had to be learned gradually and painfully. Every so often the history even of a small country throws up a person of extraordinary singleness of mind and purpose. Such a person, as Professor Gordon Donaldson reminded this Society six years ago, was William Wallace. Such also were Knox and Melville. Such, without any cavil, was Andrew Fletcher. Men and women of this calibre do not often enjoy serene and happy lives — the very fact that they cannot be deflected necessarily involves them in collisions, in sair dunts. The very fact that they see with a clarity denied to most of us means that they will suffer disappointment when their fellow mortals prove weak, timid, corruptible or just plain thrawn. They tend to be angular and prickly, and Fletcher was certainly that. The first thing, indeed, which it is right to remind ourselves about the man is that while we might have liked him, might even have loved him, and would assuredly have admired and respected him, most of us would have found him extremely difficult to work with or even to get on with. Proud, touchy, quick-tempered, rash, he would have alternately infuriated and saddened his friends, let alone his opponents. For Fletcher was quintessentially independent, wholly incapable — I myself would say admirably incapable — of being a party politician. In a modern legislative assembly he would be the despair of the Whips, always supposing that he would accept the whip of government or opposition. 'The *via di mezzo* was always ruinous,' he wrote to his brother, 'The Torys and Jacobites are idiots and madmen. And the Whig party are some of them traitors to their country and others half-witted.' That, I suppose, is simply another way of saying that he would find no place in any modern parliament save, ironically, in some hereditary or otherwise non-elective chamber which he would have despised.

Fletcher might have exasperated us in a deeper sense than with regard to mere quirks of temperament. Devoted as he was to the cause of individual liberty, he was no democrat. Almost all his recorded political utterances breathe the spirit of the small, independent, freeholding landowner. Men ought, he said, to be dispersed over the world in greater or lesser numbers, according to the goodness of the soil, and live in a more free and manly way — every man (presumably) a yeoman or bonnet laird, standing on his own feet, fending for himself. Although Fletcher was capable of broad humanity and compassion, there is little evidence that he ever rose above the inherited outlook and attitudes of the class of lowland lairds in which he had been born and reared. Steeped as he was in history, he seems not to have grasped that the lairds and freeholders of Scotland had had to contend with monarchs often tempted into tyranny and with rich and powerful nobles accustomed to uncritical deference before they could win such liberty as they possessed in Fletcher's own days. The lairds' class had not always enjoyed the decisive and determining influence in Scots affairs which at a number of major crises — 1560, 1637 and 1689 among them — it had brought to bear. A man's notion of a commonwealth or political society is sometimes grasped better by perceiving what he excludes rather than by appreciating what he takes for granted. Highlanders, criminals, vagabonds, the poor in general, starving in the prolonged dearth of the 1690s — none of these categories formed part of Fletcher's political nation of free men. Indeed, a note of contempt is surely not far removed from his gibe that in 1703 the Court Party dangled the offer of trade with the English colonies before parliament 'to mislead the commissioners of burghs, who for the most part are for anything that bears the name of trade, though but a sham, as this was.'

We must therefore take our Fletcher as we find him, and for some of us the warts included in the portrait may be too much to stomach. Although he earnestly wished 'all mankind to be as happy as the imperfections of human nature will admit', he was no Benthamite. Although he wished to see society 'attended with a more equal distribution of riches than trade and commerce will allow', he was no socialist. For, above all, Fletcher was concerned with justice and injustice, justice between individuals, justice between nations, and justice between regions — not, I think, social classes — within nations. Justice meant more to him than 'interest' or 'advantage', that is, material prosperity. Would it be rash to claim that in the 1890s Fletcher would have been pro-Boer, because for him a British conquest of the Orange Free State and Transvaal would have sprung from and created injustice? Would it be equally rash to claim that in the current argument for and against applying economic sanctions to South Africa Fletcher would have favoured sanctions because of the inherent and palpable injustice of the latterday Boer regime, rather than support the maintenance of full trade because this at least provided the oppressed with some degree of material wellbeing? 'The light of nature' he remarked, with reference to the English oppression of Ireland, 'teaches that men ought not to use one another unjustly on any account, much less under the specious pretext of government.'

Fletcher believed passionately that rulers should not tyrannize over their subjects — 'princes were made for the good government of nations, and not the government of nations framed for the private advantage of princes.' He believed with equal force that nations should not tyrannize over other nations. The mere fact that compared with Scotland England was much richer and more powerful was for him no justification for the oppression of the Scots by the English, any more than the English conquest of Ireland excused the much worse English oppression not only of the native Irish but even of the English and (by Fletcher's time) increasingly Scots colony established on Irish soil in the wake of conquest.

Fletcher's understanding of history and his lively appreciation of the political geography of Europe, much of it gained from first-hand experience, meant that he was proof against all chauvinist absurdities whether Scots, English or of any other nationality. His nationalism was far from being of the 'my country right or wrong' variety, and indeed he would have deeply despised the abdication of independent judgement implicit in such a slogan. In short, Fletcher, though not a party man, was a Whig. His whiggishness was so extreme, so pure, that it was usual for his enemies to call him a republican. What could be more whiggish than the famous 'twelve points' upon which in 1703 he insisted before the Scottish royal succession could be allowed to conform to that already adopted in England? Annual parliaments with voting by ballot; each new peerage creation to be matched by a new elected shire member;

voting in parliament restricted to actual members, no royal officials present; no royal veto on legislation; government between sessions of parliament to be controlled by a committee elected by parliament; declarations of war and peacemaking to be with parliament's consent; royal offices and pensions to be granted only by parliament; a popular militia; no standing army, and no general pardons, without consent of parliament; no judge to be allowed to sit in parliament, which would appoint the chief members of the judiciary; and finally automatic forfeiture of the throne by any sovereign who transgressed any of these points.

It may well be argued that these twelve points, if not in themselves amounting to democracy, constituted a programme of prerequisites for a democratic polity. They were informed by the principle that government derives its authority solely from the consent of the governed. And it may well be the case that Fletcher would sooner be remembered *sub specie aeternitatis* for his unflinching advocacy of the equal and indefeasible rights of the citizen against the pretensions and oppressions of kings and queens, tyrants and jacks-in-office. But here, on this occasion and in this gathering, we remember Fletcher as a patriot, whose generous soul, as Lockhart of Carnwath put it, could not endure the thought of England's domineering over Scotland. As far as his published speeches and writings are concerned, there is an unresolved ambiguity in Fletcher's attitude towards the autonomy of his native land. On the one hand he took a staunchly traditional 'historic' view, fortified by a thorough and impressive grounding in the history of Scotland and its neighbours. This view clearly accepted the immemorial right of the Scots to exist as a separate nation, even expressed at one point with an echo of the Declaration of Arbroath; 'the Scots, who have for so many ages, with such resolution, defended their liberty against the Picts, Britons, Romans, Saxons, Danes, Irish, Normans and English.' But in his discussion with Sir Christopher Musgrave, Sir Edward Seymour and the earl of Cromartie — of which, of course, we have only his own report — he opposed the union of Scotland with England as a rational pragmatist. 'Upon the union of the crowns ... though particular persons of the Scots nation had many great and profitable places at court ... yet that was no advantage to our country, which was totally neglected, like a farm managed by servants and not under the eye of the master.' 'If I make a bargain for the people that inhabit the northern part of this island, I ought principally to consider the interest of those who shall continue to live in that place, that they may find their account in the agreement, and be better provided for than they are.' For Fletcher, in modern parlance, it was not good enough to say to an aggrieved Scot 'Get on your bike and pedal off to the south east of England' — nor even 'Get in your boat and sail away to the English plantations across the Atlantic'. Moreover, Fletcher had a very acute sense, rather in advance of his own generation, of the imbalance caused even in England, never mind Britain as a whole, by the phenomenal growth of London. 'This vast city is like the head of a rickety child, which by drawing to itself the nourishment that should be distributed in due proportions to the rest of the languishing body becomes overcharged.' 'If in the union of several countries under one government, the prosperity and happiness of the different nations are not considered, as well as of the whole united body, those that are more remote from the seat of the government will only be made subservient to the interest of others, and their condition very miserable.'

Fletcher was thus a regionalist as well as a nationalist, and in upholding the immemorial rights of his own small nation — as indeed he would have upheld with equal fervour the rights of other small nations — he wished to decentralize government and administration. In the long view, it can hardly be said that his predictions about the effects of union of 1707 have been wholly falsified. Admittedly, compared with 1707, the Scotland of 1985 is five times as populous and enormously (though not calculably) more prosperous. But Scotland in 1985 must be compared with England, Europe and the rest of the world in 1985, not just with itself three hundred years ago. The exponential accumulation of wealth, investment and population in the Southern half, especially

the south-eastern segment of England — though it was offset for a
century and a half by the coal and iron based Industrial Revolution
— has now for several generations taken a course which Fletcher
envisaged. What might have surprised him is the survival of an
identifiable Scotland along with an identifiable England. In the
official relations of England and Scotland over the past century or
so — as distinct from the *de facto* relations — two strands may be
discerned. The first stems from the constitutional and legal
provisions of the Treaty of Union, whereby the continued and
distinct existence of the kingdoms of England and Scotland was
recognised, although each was to be subsumed within the novel
entity of a 'United Kingdom'. It has been in line with this strand
that the history of law and of the churches has taken a markedly
different course in each country. In our own times it has been in
line with this strand that institutions of great value in national
life, such as the Scottish Land Court, the National Library of
Scotland, the Register House and its national archives, the National
Trust and this honourable Society meeting here today, have been
set up and have met with notable success. The second strand has
been that of 'devolution', which has tended to ignore the
fundamental constitutional basis of the 1707 union and instead to
envisage the gracious delegation of administrative and (to a limited
extent) political powers from the centre. It was of course this strand
which was activated a century ago with the establishment of the
Scottish secretaryship, and it is this strand which has held sway in
the field of education. Against these two quite distinct yet at times
converging strands have been ranged, ever since 1707 but much more
powerfully since the end of the first World War, the forces of
centralisation and remote control, in general legislation, in overseas
relations, in industry and commerce, and, perhaps most strikingly
of all, in the sensitive and immensely influential field of radio and
television, where the failure to establish anything which might be
called a national Scottish organisation for the communication of
news, current affairs, public debate, the arts and entertainment is
surely the most astonishing single feature in the collective life of

twentieth-century Scotland. Neither of the two strands I have
mentioned has been able, it seems to me, to do anything more than
partially arrest the de-industrialisation of Scotland which has been
a most conspicuous feature of our history in the past thirty or forty
years. It might be objected that as mass industry came to Scotland
only, as it were, by accident, we cannot seriously object if it
disappears by default. It was precisely against this fatalism that
Fletcher of Saltoun attempted to warn his countrymen during the
debates on the union of 1707. The full realisation of coal and iron,
the potential in textiles and of course the undersea oil resources
now being depleted were all beyond his imagining, and he could
claim no more than the modest advantages of fisheries and foreign
trade. Yet, as he said, 'a distinct sovereignty does always enable a
people to retain some riches, and leaves them without excuse if
they do not rise to considerable wealth.' There is still much that
we may learn from Fletcher's sturdy example. The Saltire Society,
which he would surely have approved, does right to cherish his
memory. And just as the kirk of Alvie would have been apt for the
commemoration of Thomas Randolph, his fellow patriot from an
earlier age, so this parish kirk of Saltoun, where Fletcher lies buried,
is the most fitting spot for our act of commemoration today.

1986

Republicanism, Fletcher and Ferguson

Neil MacCormick

Sir Neil MacCormick MEP, has been Regius Professor of Public Law at the University of Edinburgh since 1972, and was Vice Principal between 1997 and 1999. He has been a Member of the European Parliament (SNP) for Scotland since 1999. His publications include *Questioning Sovereignty* (1999)

Republicanism: Fletcher and Ferguson

Neil MacCormick

Andrew Fletcher of Saltoun was 'a Scotch gentleman of great parts and many virtues, but a most violent republican and extravagantly passionate', according to Bishop Burnet. Certainly, one theme that surfaces very quickly in any study of Fletcher's work is the idea of a republic. This is not merely a matter of interest in the republican form of government. It also concerns the spirit and the special virtues thought to be inherent in, required by, and best realizable through such a form of government. Why, however, should one link forms of govermnent and virtues associated with them? The answer can be found in the way sundry eighteenth-century political thinkers criticised the tendency toward absolutism or despotism that they discerned in the kingdoms of their period. The case for limited or constitutional monarchy was commonly thought to be this: as *monarchy*, it enshrined sufficient authority to enable firm and expeditious dispatch of the business of state. As *limited*, by means of laws and of a requirement to be answerable before legislatures representative and partially democratic in form, it opened sufficient space for individual human liberty in a political sense. It procured, in short, the best available balance of authority and freedom.

But why did liberty matter? Why, indeed, *does* it matter? One can answer such a question in at least three ways. One way is to assert a natural right to freedom, saying that every person is born free and should remain so, without suffering violence or confinement at the hands of others. The essential truth of this need not be doubted, but the trouble remains, as everyone knows, that life in civil society involves some departure from full natural right, and the question is, 'how much?'. A second way is to appeal to private interest — to say that people like being free and can maximize their own good if free to pursue it. The problem here is to balance my freedom to pursue my interest against my need for certain protections from violence and misfortune, and to know what that balance should be. A third is to respond in terms of public good and civic virtue — to argue that free human beings best realize their humanity by acting as free members of a body politic and by identifying their good with its good. People best realize themselves in making their best possible contribution to the common good of a political community in which they have the opportunity for independent action. This view has its own difficulties, but it is the one I shall mainly consider here.

Fletcher insisted, in the aftermath of the revolution of 1688-89, that the Scots Parliament should acquire and use the power to withhold public funds until the queen's government joined in enacting its laws. He further proposed that her ministers should be elected by and answerable to Parliament. By the standards of his times, such proposals were flatly republican. (We do well to be reminded that republicanism in the relevant sense does not preclude the possibility of favouring a hereditary headship of state).

His vigorous opposition to the Articles of Union proposed by the Scottish and English commissioners for the constituting of a United Kingdom of Great Britain in 1707, subject to the required enabling legislation of the English and Scottish parliaments (which thereby abolished themselves), brought another element in his republicanism to the fore. He foresaw that the incorporating form of union would remove from Scotland all independence of political initiative, depriving it of that theatre of representative politics in which, he considered, civic virtue and the opportunity for dedication to the public good of one's community can alone be realized. He and others who pleaded in that debate for confederation rather than union, appealing to the good of part and whole alike, lost the vote, even if perhaps they won the argument.

Some of what they argued has had lasting resonance in relation to the American constitutional debate.

Such pleas were grounded in a view of Scottish constitutional history and the experience of Western European kingdoms, a view that goes back at least as far as the sixteenth-century humanist George Buchanan and his celebrated book *De Iure Regni Apud Scotos* (1579). That text asserted and argued for the right of the Scots to depose their chosen kings or — much to the point of the recent deposition of Mary Queen of Scots — queens, if ever they betrayed the trust consensually reposed in them by the people, thereby taking on the character of tyrants rather than that of lawful rulers. This conception of the liberty of the community, even subject to institutions of limited monarchy, is all-important to what I am calling the republican ideal.

It is also important to the background of the greatest of Scots legal writings, James Dalrymple Viscount Stair's *Institutions of the Law of Scotland.* That book sets out a theory of law erected on the basis of a contractual theory of the state. From this by no means original starting point he developed a strikingly original account of private law. Such law in a civilized community is, he claimed, founded on personal freedom and is aimed at the securing of 'society, property and commerce'. This idea of law matches ideas in Locke so closely that one can in a way treat Stair's *Institutions* as almost a companion volume to the *Two Treatises of Government* by Locke.

Some would doubtless correct me for ascribing Stair and Locke to the same intellectual tradition as Fletcher and his like. Stair and Locke, it might be argued, belong more to early or emergent liberalism than to the republican tradition, whether that be traced back to roots only in Buchanan or (as would be more proper) to the theorists of the medieval Italian city-republics and their seventeenth-century revivals by thinkers such as James Harrington. This is indeed an important point. Unquestionably, Stair and Locke stress something like the natural rights view of liberty as qualified also by the appeal to interest. Their idea is of law and government upholding natural liberty and fostering the conditions of general well-being through an established system of property and commerce. Here they foreshadow the economic liberalism of Adam Smith and his successors, rather than echoing the civic virtue theme of the republican tradition. Even so, the liberties they advocate are not dissimilar to the different strands of the various republican arguments. And even as late as Smith, the characteristic stoic and republican virtue of self-command remains an important shot in the liberal locker.

However that may be, we can certainly find a difference between Fletcher and Stair or, rather, Stair's personal and political descendants, in respect of the union debate in the opening decade of the eighteenth century. For Fletcher and his like, the incorporation of Scotland into an essentially English Great Britain meant its end as a theatre of civic virtue. It meant the spiriting away of leading figures to a distant capital and the consequent impoverishment not only of local talent and ability but of local economic strength as well. The real argument on the other side was for peace, free trade, and the firmer preservation both in Scotland and in England of the individual, religious, and political liberties of the revolution settlement of 1688-89. Here, perhaps, we may ascribe a difference of political preference directly to the opposition of values between republicanism and proto-liberalism. At least, one can discern deeply held differences in perspective as to what counts as the flourishing and well-being of individuals and communities.

This dispute involves, even if it is not reducible to, a difference of opinion on the optimal size of a free society. Fletcher wanted to keep political communities manageably small and to build a regard for the public good upon the sense of loyalty to community, which the ancient tradition of small polities fosters. Against him, it was argued that the enlarged theatre created for the pursuit of commercial advantage outweighed the advantages he claimed for his preferred outcome and that, in any event, loyalties could as well be transferred to the new union as kept narrowly to the old kingdom. The counterargument, that a federation could procure the commercial advantages without the other losses, hardly got off the ground once it was clear that the English were not interested in that alternative.

The theory of smallness as favorable to liberty continued as a theme of republican thought into the high period of the Enlightenment, certainly in Scotland. Its classic representative is Adam Ferguson, professor of moral philosophy in Edinburgh and, as the author of *An Essay on the History of Civil Society* (1767), one of the founders of sociology. In that work, Ferguson returns again and again to the theme of the liberty enjoyed in the Greek and Italian civic republics of antiquity and to the personal and communal virtues that arose from the intense identification that polities of that kind fostered between individual and community. There, he argued, was none of the servility or dependence such as arises in the courts of absolute monarchs or in lesser cases of patronage and clientage. Citizens made independent contributions to the commonweal out of their own commitment to it and their own judgment of what it required.

Whereas critics of republicanism were usually apt to argue that small republics, are always internally factious and externally warlike, Ferguson turned these arguments upside down. The problem of faction he regarded as grossly exaggerated. The good emerges not from bland consensus but, like truth, from the vigorous dissensus of passionate debate. The end should not be the extinguishment of faction but the securing of pluralism and overall equilibrium among factions. It is from the tension among vigorously held and hard-won contentions that a real conception of and regard for public good emerges. Such a spirit is also essential to the preservation of individual and political liberty. Only the insistence on one's right to put forward one's own view or that of one's party could guarantee the preservation of personal freedom and freedom of public action. Liberty resides more in civic spirit than in laws, however admirably framed. Here one finds a striking antinomianism, an outspoken mistrust of laws as alone sufficient (if even necessary) to the preservation of liberty. To become dependent on a specialized class of lawyers and judges who are the only ones able to find their way through the thickets of legal enactment or entrenchment of rights is, says Ferguson, a poor kind of freedom, for it substitutes one kind of dependency for another. It is worse indeed if one's freedom and estate depend on the whims of a despot rather than on the labyrinths of legal interpretation as conducted by experts, but neither is the optimal condition of humanity.

As with internal faction, so too with external enmities. Peace at any price is not the goal. After all, says Ferguson, it is in warfare that some of the finer traits of human nature come into their own. Here are found courage and self-sacrifice for one's friends, here the virtues of patriotism and the exaltation of public over private good. Moreover, even in times of peace, the spirit of emulation and rivalry that characterizes small republics in relation to each other is more apt to call forth ingenuity and inventiveness than is soporific peace over extensive kingdoms. So even if it is true that republican liberties require small states rather than large empires, that is no disadvantage. The creation of extensive empires, necessarily involving strong central power, is inimical to the higher forms of human good.

These higher forms of good are by no means to be defined in economic or materialist terms. It is not by leafing around, enjoying the fruits of materialistic enterprise, that humans find their good or even their happiness. To be human is to be active. No sooner is work over than play begins, and the favored forms of play are yet more violent and active than most forms of work. This point may, of course, suggest a certain detachment on Ferguson's part from the praises his contemporaries were wont to heap upon the emergence of a commercial society out of earlier and more barbarous epochs. Ferguson was perhaps the first to notice the fiction of the Hobbesian state of nature as a supposed representation of some presocial condition of humanity. It is the commercial form of society, Ferguson notes, that encourages humans to see each other in instrumental terms rather than as ends in themselves. The solitariness of human beings is at its greatest not in the most primitive but rather in the most advanced forms of human society. The problem for commercial societies is to sustain social solidarity and public spirit. And here they face special difficulties, given the ways in which their economic forms lead persons to relate to one another.

It is certainly not difficult to find in Ferguson's advocacy of these views a precursor of certain aspects of Jeffersonian republicanism. The regard for an upright class of independent yeoman farmers, the mistrust of commerce and commercialism, the cool view of lawyers as a class are all opinions that a Virginian republican might warmly endorse. The thesis that 'the right of the people to keep and bear arms shall not be infringed' is one that we can readily imagine striking a chord in the breast of a Ferguson.

Again, though, it needs to be remarked that Fletcher of Saltoun was one of the more vigorous earlier advocates of the view that the collapse of the old feudal militia had been a prerequisite for the rise of royal absolutism. He was among the more persuasive of the late-seventeenth-century advocates of the restoration of liberty through re-establishment of a militia as the chief national defence force. In this and in other ways, some of them rebarbative to our modern sensibilities, Fletcher made himself the spokesman of the idea of the active citizen engaged in the defence of his community, taking its politics seriously, and insisting on limitations upon all political officeholders, even the highest.

There was more to be said about republicanism than he said. The tale was carried on by Ferguson and doubtless others. But when we gather to celebrate a great patriot, we can even to this day ally ourselves to aspects of his constitutional thought. We are all democrats now, and it befits us to think in what ways a democratic and republican form of government connects up to certain distinctive virtues, and to those aspects of human nature in respect of which we are at our most human.

1987

The Relevance of Fletcher of Saltoun

Bruce Lenman

Bruce P. Lenman is Senior Lecturer in Modem History, at St Andrews University. His publications include: *An Economic History of Modern Scotland* (1977), *The Jacobite Risings in Britain 1689-1746* (1980), *The Jacobite Cause* (1986), *The Eclipse of Parliament* (1992).

The Relevance of Fletcher of Saltoun

Bruce Lenman

Ladies and gentlemen; we are assembled here to commemorate the life of and work of a man born in 1653 who died in 1716. His final illness began in Paris, it is said from the after-effects of drinking the water of the Seine. His nephew, then a student at the Dutch university of Leiden hastened to his side in Paris and tried to bear him home here to Saltoun. He expired on the journey home in London on September 15, and came back here, the parish kirk of his ancestral barony, in his coffin to be laid amongst his predecessors as lairds of Saltoun in the family vault below this kirk. Thus ended the life of one whose biographer described him as sprung 'on one side of Royal blood, and on the other side, of gentle and distinguished stock'. He is remembered, in so far as he is remembered, as a deeply conservative patriotic Scottish laird of unimpeachable integrity. The Whig secret serviceman Macky summed him up as 'a gentleman steady in his principles, of nice honour, with abundance of learning, brave as the sword he wears, and bold as a lion. He would lose his life readily to serve his country, and would not do a base thing to save it'. These sentiments were fully endorsed from the other end of the political spectrum by the Jacobite George Lockhart of Carnwath, who like Fletcher took a decidedly hostile view of the Act of Union of 1707.

It is perhaps unfortunate that Andrew Fletcher of Saltoun is thus remembered primarily as an unsuccessful Scottish patriot. Since the Union went through, his life can be seen as ending in failure, and with the passage of time he has become more and more an inhabitant of a distant and alien country — the Past — with little to show us save the enduring moral message of a sterling character.   To think in this way is natural.   It is also deeply and absolutely wrong. Fletcher of Saltoun's ideas are often, though of course not always, as relevant today as when they were first articulated by him, and that for two reasons. One is that the man was, like all great men, a complex being who can be viewed validly from several different angles.   In the popular caricature of the principled opponent of legislation passed in 1707 we lose far too easily other sides of Fletcher of Saltoun's thought, sides which are actually more important because unlike a given political episode, they are not caught in time like a fly in amber: they are concerned with eternal issues like the maintenance of and the threats to, a free government for a free people. That is one of my two main themes in this discourse which I have the honour and privilege of delivering to you today — the contemporary relevance of much of Andrew Fletcher of Saltoun's thought. My second theme is not entirely different or separated from my first, but it is distinct enough to be articulated in its own right: we totally delude ourselves if we think that we have left behind us the problems and threats which so disturbed him.   On the contrary, they have within our polity reared their ugly heads on a scale which Fletcher would probably have thought inconceivable.   His central concern was with the problem of the over-mighty executive scheming and plotting to subvert the political structures of a free society. If asked to cite an example of the sort of undesirable, centralised absolutist executive tyranny capable of growing out of a long process of successful prosecution of such subversion, he would almost certainly have cited the panoplistic absolutism of Louis XIV, the contemporary Sun King of France. But the effective power of Louis XIV to coerce and bully the other twenty million Frenchmen of his day was in practice vastly more limited than the capacity of any post 1945 British Prime Minister to coerce and rally the 50,000,000 or so inhabitants of the United Kingdom.   Mrs Thatcher disposes not only of absolute centralised power (or sovereignty to use the polite but misleading term often used to mask the reality) but she also disposes of a vast and subservient bureaucracy in every corner of her realm. Louis XIV had very few civil servants and he could not fire the great majority of people holding royal offices of profit. His executive was heavily armed, as is ours, but his police forces were minute, and have been described by one recent scholar as basically an exercise in bluff. Our government disposes of a vast police organisation, which not only possesses technical devices for surveillance inconceivable in the late seventeenth century, but also appears to have firearms freely and routinely available to it. One could go on to talk of our secret police structures such as MI5, MI6 and the CIA but that is a separate issue best mentioned later. Louis XIV may have once said 'l'état c'est moi' but in practice he could not hope to rule the provinces of Old France (each with its distinctive provincial code of customary law — Les Coutumes) without the cooperation of the local elites. Compared with Mrs Thatcher — or even Harold Wilson or Ted Heath — Louis XIV was a roi fainéant.

Yet do remember that the political legitimacy of the central British political power-structure rested in the latter part of the life of Fletcher of Saltoun on the same basis on which, in theory, it rests now — the Glorious Revolution of 1688. Fletcher had good reason to remember well the absolutist pretensions of Charles II and of JamesVII and II, from whose wrath he fled abroad, returning to fight both in the Duke of Monmouth's ill-fated and in many ways surprisingly radical Western Rising against James in 1685, and again with William of Orange's more fortunate invasion of 1688. Currently our rulers are arranging a rather low-key celebration of the Revolution in 1988, its 300th Anniversary, on the specious grounds that they do not wish to stir up passions in Ulster — as if they could either stir or quiet that province! Look forward ladies and gentlemen to some rather uninspired oratory with much emphasis on 300 years of gloriously happy Anglo-Dutch co-operation, which is not really the point at all. The point is that the Revolution saw a transfer of sovereignty from the Crown, to which it had always appertained, to the King in his Westminster

Parliament and the justification (for an exercise which the exiled Stewarts regularly denounced as offensive to the laws of God and Man) was that only by such a transfer could an incipient executive tyranny be permanently bridled into the happy format of a 'mixed' government combining elements of monarchy, aristocracy and democracy, so wisely and delicately balanced against one another that the frail plant of Liberty, one which grows best in the interstices of complex, interlocked political structures might flower gloriously in the happiest and best of all governments known to 18th century Britons as 'Our Happy Constitution in Church and State'.

It is perhaps just as well that our present rulers do not wish to have too much discussion in public as to how much of that happy, balanced constitution survives, for the only possible answer is Nothing. British government is not balanced, nor 'happy' in the eighteenth century sense, nor have we a constitution, written or unwritten. This fact has been apparent to perceptive foreign observers for most of this century. As one Frenchman said, a very long time ago 'En Angleterre la Constitution peut se changer de minute en minute où plutôt ça n'existe pas'. Where government believes that its vital interests are at stake, I even have doubts whether the Rule of Law really exists. We may be grateful that MI5 and MI6 appear to be full of people who are not only of the extreme paranoid right in their politics, but also quite unbelievably incompetent. I have a friend whose office phone appears to have been tapped regularly during the miners' strike because he was writing a refutation of some of the NCB's statistics. The perpetrators of the tapping were so incompetent that he says they could be heard in the background on the line uttering such deathless remarks as "Got that down on tape Bert?" When the fracas was over and they went away we considered sending a letter to Maggie complaining that life was not the same without them. Much more serious than such idiot cantraips are the allegations that Stephen Ward was in fact framed by the Home Secretary and the police during the Profumo Scandal, an allegation which is not only formidably documented but also persuasive, in that it makes much more sense of a confusing affair that any alternative version. The fact that the knee-jerking response of Her Majesty's Government is to try and protect its minions 'right or wrong' and to suppress discussion by means of the Official Secrets Act is unfortunate. It is conceivable that government is innocent of some of the charges levelled against it, but it behaves like a guilty party virtually every time.

Would Fletcher of Saltoun have been surprised had he been granted a brief return to the world of affairs, say this year, and someone pointed out to him that he was in a land ruled by the most excessively secretive of Western governments whose Official Secrets Act is not so much a scandal as a stench in the nostrils of any sincere democrat (and I may say, exposed for the evil conspiracy it is by the admirably positive approach to freedom of information in the USA). Not at all. Fletcher lived through the late seventeenth-century Scottish Watergate — the inquiry into the Massacre of Glencoe, in the course of which King Billy mulishly defended his guilty servants. Generations of subsequent historians have lavished thousands of pages on the 'Romantic' Jacobite and clan dimensions of a botched job which cost 36 lives. Fletcher was assiduously clear about the important issues. This sort of violence was the way King James VII's administration had behaved in the Highlands, and Kings William's cover-up for the guilty men, often the same who had served James VII, raised the very real question of whether the Revolution had made any difference. The answer is, of course, that there was always an element of ambiguity in the Revolution. William of Orange was more Stewart in blood than Orange and he came not to save the Brits from King James, but to save what he could of late Stewart monarchical power from the extraordinary political stupidity of King James, which threatened to ruin all, and might be the harbinger of another radical Commonwealth experiment like that of the 1650s.

The word Commonwealth did not frighten Fletcher of Saltoun, but then he <u>was</u> a Commonwealthman or Real Whig and as Robert

Viscount Molesworth, his good friend said in the Preface to his 1721 edition of *Franco-Gallia* 'A True Whig is not afraid of the name of a Commonwealthman, because so many foolish People, who know not what it means run it down'. On the contrary, Fletcher was proud to belong to that active minority of True Whigs who in the generation after the Glorious Revolution tried to preserve its political gains from the creeping counter-revolution built into the very earliest of post-Revolution administrations, and to extend the benefits of that Glorious Revolution to wider categories of fellow Britons. Fletcher was always clear and tough minded. When one thinks of the reams of egregious drivel churned out on behalf of the cause of the indefeasible hereditary right of the Stewarts, and the way in which blind obedience to monarchical authority was assiduously identified with the security of property and the stability of the social system (to the point where many Englishmen could only bring themselves to live with the necessary exclusion of the Old Pretender from power by embracing the absurd story that he was no son of James VII or II but a supposititious child) it is a relief to read Fletcher's letter from Paris to his nephew on February 20, 1716, in which Fletcher remarks that anyone disposed to doubt the Old Pretender's genetic relationship with the Stewarts has only to look at the total mess into which the Jacobite rebellion has fallen during James Francis Edward Stewart's one and a half months in Scotland to see that he really is his father's son.

Fletcher was always emphatic that free governments were perpetually endangered by 'corruption', which he would have defined in two ways, both very active in Anglo-American political society today. One is the endless conspiracy of executive government to escape its due and reasonable limits. This is a problem even in America where the vocabulary of the True Whigs became the normal mode of discourse in the thirteen provinces of the English nation which seceded in 1775 to start to form a new nationality, and whose subsequent constitution duly embodies most of those formal systems of checks and balances and guarantees of rights which a True Whig would regard as desirable, and which are now the supreme glory of the fifty states, the palladium of their liberties, and of their prosperity. As a senior Congressman said recently in connection with the endless Iranscam revelations 'There cannot be a functioning, respected democracy in this country as long as members of the Executive Branch habitually come before committees of the Congress and lie'. Yet by British standards, the Americans have comparatively little to complain of. They have all the checks and balances still in place. We have none.

Fletcher was not necessarily an opponent of a form of British Union. In the late seventeenth century he thought such a Union might be the saving of Scottish liberties from Jacobite counter-revolution. However, he did object very strongly to the incorporating package rammed through in 1707, not least because it vastly increased the power of the executive by placing at their disposal the subservient squad of Scots MPs and Scots so-called Representative Peers (most of the latter in effect nominated on a government list and notorious for servility). All recent research suggests unequivocally that the 42 Scots MPs after 1707, a few mavericks apart, were the first modern MPs. They were elected but not representative and the manly independence of a significant proportion of English back-benchers meant nothing to them. They went to Westminster to curry favour with and secure jobs from the executive. They were the first phalanx of well-whipped cannon fodder a PM could simply order through the appropriate lobby. As for the bringing forward of Scottish issues, needs, or demands . . . that was unthinkable. It would simply annoy an executive that already over-busy not solving a whole range of problems from Ireland to America to Bengal. Now , of course, we have reached the point where any government with a majority of ten or more can just ignore the House of Commons. I think it was Bob Boothby who once said that in 30 odd years around that place he only ever saw one vote that made any difference to anything that mattered — and that was one which every recent PM would probably have ignored, for Chamberlain resigned because his majority fell, not because he lost a vote. The rituals of the House are a farcical waste of time, and people like Des Wilson are quite right to suggest that opposition MPs should simply regard it as a handy perpetual campaign base. Pity any intelligent Tory survivor amongst the cab-load of the faithful left in the Scottish seats if he has no job. The House is a rubber-stamp. The Whips are happy for you never to be there if you are paired. Without Maggie's patronage life is meaningless.

Fletcher could not have foreseen the party machines which have produced this result, and he whose acquaintance was of an aristocratic cast (is not his *Account of a Conversation Concerning a Right Regulation of Governments for the Common Good of Mankind* in the form of a letter to the Marquis of Montrose, and the Earls of Rothes, Roxburgh and Haddington), would probably simply not believe the lunatic basis of our current second chamber. It is all summed up by NATO secretary — General Viscount Carrington who, when taunted with his own hereditary peerage (he is the descendant of Mr Smith, Pitt's banker) replied devastatingly to the serried ranks of life peers 'At least I represent my father. All you lot represent is Prime Ministerial patronage'. Now it is generally said that debate in the second chamber is superior to that in the Commons — an appalling comment on the Commons — but when all is said and done a nation is deeply degraded when what should be one of the watch-dogs of its liberties is turned into a Prime-Ministerial poodle, a dumping ground for embarrassing alcoholics like the late George Brown; a premier's (admittedly very intelligent) lady friend; Wets whom Maggie wants rid of; the inevitable collection of unsuccessful university vice-chancellors and wealthy contributors to party funds, not to mention your ennobled trade union leaders who sold out either their party or their members the year before they retired to the House of Lords, metamorphosed from Bert Sprocket of the Amalgamated Offshore Riveters to Lord Fanshawe of Finchley in the former GLC area.

What would not have surprised Fletcher at all in our political scene would be the ferocious assault on local government, once one of the glories of the English political tradition, now broken and trampled on, and nowhere more than here in North Britain, where the mini-dictatorship of the Secretary of State, itself a pale reflection of a greater tyranny elsewhere, has acquired powers which effectively abolish any meaningful local government autonomy in a nation where the current Secretary of State represents not just a small and disliked minority, but even a smallish minority of the votes cast in the constituency he represents. None of this is surprising. Lord Hailsham summed its origins up with typical trenchancy and clarity a few years ago in a lecture in St Andrews where he pointed out that with a legislature totally dominated by the executive through a party system (which, thanks to a peculiar voting system, can deliver absolute power to the party leader on the back of about 40% of the votes cast at an election) and our poisonous doctrine of absolute sovereignty (which is and should be an attribute of God alone) we do not live in a Democracy so much as in an Elective Dictatorship. How wise his words were. (What we who cheered them did not realise is that what truly distressed him then about the system was that Harold Wilson was in charge of it.)

Given the nature of the British minority-based elective dictatorship, it is hardly surprising that one of its great achievements has been geographical polarisation and alienation on a scale unprecedented since the better part of the English nation declared its independence in 1776. The present government has absolutely no support in Ulster, virtually none in Scotland and Wales and precious little in England north of the M36. The deeply alien nature of the regime can be sensed by anyone in a room anywhere North or West of the Tory South-East heartland when Our Glorious Leader opens her mouth on TV or Radio. Three syllables are enough, or rather three of those syllables are more than enough.

There was always a very British side to Fletcher. His Commonwealth circle was led by an Irish nobleman, Molesworth, and Fletcher was always on speaking terms with the English Whig lords. Through the Ulsterman Francis Hutchison, Commonwealth

principles entered standard Scottish academic discourse, for
Hutchison was Professor of Moral Philosophy at Glasgow, a
university blessed then and now with many outstanding professors
from the North of Ireland. His pupils included Adam Smith whose
reactionary political spirit would clearly have liked to challenge
basic Commonwealth principles, but who instead, with his equally
reactionary friend David Hume, could only dare subtly to seek to
undermine them. Fletcher was interested in a federal union, since
small independent states would have great difficulty surviving in
the British Isles. Molesworth advocated something similar in the
Preface of *Franco-Gallia* and may have been influenced by Fletcher
in his views.   Certainly Fletcher expected a just British Federal
Union to make due provision for the decentralization of government
and to prevent such injustices as were being inflicted on Ireland,
and even remedy 'the great imperfections and inconveniences of
Wales'.

The greatest, the most urgent and the most important task facing
the British peoples in the remaining years of this century is the
irreversible destruction of the absolute monarchy in the unworthy
hands of successive premiers.   To that monarch the glitzy façade
of the nominal Royals acts as a sort of farcical cache-sexe. If anyone
doubts the accuracy of 'fig-leaf' as a description for the nominal
wearer of the crown, let them ask themselves how effective is a
monarch who let Harold Wilson's last Honours List through,
despite the anguished protests of the appropriate vetting
committee, which quite rightly said it stank. If Fletcher of Saltoun
were alive today he would certainly argue that a Scottish Assembly
was now the only way forward from the one-person misgovernment
of the modern UK.   But he would not want it merely as a sop to
Cerberus — a grudging concession to Scots whom the government
means to treat like Ulstermen and push them out of the system if
they continue to argue. He would want it for all the British peoples,
as part of a fully federal UK. And that is what we should fight for:
not a fresh layer of government as Mr Rifkind deludes himself. He
must go. So must his office. So must a significant part of his

bureaucracy. Meaningful devolved assemblies must have a solid tax-base but not in the shape of additional taxes — gathered in the shape of revenue taken irreversibly away from the central government, whose general range of powers must be sharply reduced. And since the experience of centuries since 1716 wholly confirms Fletcher's deeply-held conviction that any executive will scheme and plot endlessly and absolutely unscrupulously to concentrate all power in its own (preferably irresponsible) hands, we need to secure our new-won liberties with a written constitution, a Supreme Court, a meaningful, elected second chamber at the centre, and a patriated Bill of Rights available to Britons in the U.K at reasonable costs. Lord Acton's slightly misquoted remark that 'Power corrupts and absolute power corrupts absolutely', represents a logical summation of Fletcher's approach to the problem of the over-mighty executive, and it states starkly a great truth. Centralised absolutism in the UK must not be <u>modified</u> — it must be <u>broken</u>, for the sake of all Britons. Let us join what eighteenth-century men of a liberal cast of mind called 'the party of Humanity' and rise against it, drawing inspiration from the principles of he whose mortal remains lie below us. Dust they may be, but dust he is not. If I may misquote another Scot and True Whig, John Paul Jones, the father of the American navy 'Sir, he has not yet begun to fight'.

1988

'*Ane end of ane auld Sang*'

Billy Kay

Billy Kay is a broadcaster, writer, producer and campaigner for the Scots language. He produced the Odyssey series for Radio Scotland and many other documentaries. Publications include: *Knee Deep in Claret* (with Cailean MacLean, 1983 and 1994), *Scots, the Mither Tongue* (1986) and *The Complete Odyssey* (1996).

'Ane end of ane auld sang'

Billy Kay

On April 28 1707 Chancellor Seafield brocht the last Scots pairliament to a close wi the words, 'Now, there's ane end of ane auld sang'.

Sangs, poetry, literature have aye been that closely thirled tae the Scottish identity, it was quite natural for Seafield tae bid fareweel tae the auld parliament an refer tae aw that had gane afore as a sang. Whiles, the sang wes a dowie lament, whiles a gleg rant. But, as lang as awbody could sing the sangs, sae lang as they shared the same culture, why be bothered about ocht else? That wes the idea that drave the man we're gethered here tae honour the day, Andra Fletcher o Saltoun, tae write:

> I knew a very wise man . . . [who] believed that if a man were permitted to make all the ballads, he need not care who should make the laws of a nation.

He wes richt then, an he's been richt for gey near twa hunder an fifty year sinsyne. But I'm no shuir gin he's richt nou, because the auld certainties o a shared culture are nou under greater threat than ever afore.

But until recently the ties atween the culture o the folk an the literature hiv been strang eneuch tae gar ordinary fowk feel that the artists an writers belanged tae them. It's a literary tradition gey different fae the mair rarified elitist tradition o the English — a body o evidence where 90 per cent of the witnesses are never called — is the wey Willie McIlvanney described it. In contrast, the Scots tradition has aye bidit close tae the fowk, an it's got deep ruits an a lang memory. Ony time an uncle took us oot on a drive when we were weans, inevitably we wad airt oursels towards the coast, an on cue juist afore Ayr, ma faither would mind us that we were in the area o Barnweill and gie us the words Wallace said whan he saw the great conflagration in the English military stockade situated there at the time o the Wars o Independence . . . "Burn ye weel ye Barns o' Ayr" The quote gaed back tae Blin Hary's "Wallace" but wes likely kennt by ma faither via the eichteenth century version by Hamilton o Gilbertfield that produced such a patriotic reaction in Burns. . . "the story of Wallace poured a Scottish prejudice in my veins which will boil along there till the flood-gates of life shut in eternal rest." Burns succeeded in distillin an essential Scottishness that reached oot tae aw levels o society, but he wesnae alane. The reason Sir David Lyndsay's play Ane Satyre o the Thrie Estaitis wes sae frichtsome tae thaim that held pouer in the Kirk, wes because like Burns he wes awready read an recited in the housses o puir cottar bodies an ilkie ither social groupin afore the play wes performed. That is why his wark in the Satyre garred the religious establishment tremble an fash when he turned against thaim — they kennt fowk responded to it.

   Although kennin ocht about Scottish culture wes rarely a help in social advancement in Scotland, there is a britherhood that recognises its worth. Ane of the best examples o it wes a story I heard fae a Burnsian fae my ain Irvine Valley, Willie Morrison. Comin in tae Dover efter a coachin tour o Europe, Willie wes warned by the English majority on the bus no tae tak ony chances at the Customs as they were famous for bein gey strict. Willie wesnae blate though, an decidit tae tak an extra bottle o whisky and extra packets o cigarette through wi him. Houever as he wes breengin tae the exit, ane o the offeicials cried him ower an askit him tae open his bag. As he wes daein whit he wes tellt, the offeicial noticed the address tag an said, "I see you come from Ayrshire, Sir...is it Kilmarnock?" "Naw" said Willie, "I'm fae faurer east." "Darvel?" speired the official. "Naw" said Willie . . . and launched into the openin o the Holy Fair:

Upon a simmer Sunday morn
When Nature's face is fair,

Tae Willie's surprise the offeicial continued wi the neist twa lines:

I walkèd forth to view the corn
And snuff the caller air.

By nou the haill customs hall wes agog as the pair o thaim continued
as ane:

The rising sun owre Galston muirs
Wi glorious licht was glintin;
The hares were hirplin doon the furs.
The laverocks they were chantin

An here the offeicial liftit his chalk an wi a dramatic flourish
syncopated in time wi the rhythm o the final line, marked the cases
as duty free wi fower perfect crosses:

Fu X sweet X that X day X   "On ye go Sir, a pleisure tae
welcome the likes o you intae the country!"

Whaur's yer Wullie Shakespeare Noo? An yet the anglicisers
an improvers hae the cheek tae suggest that haein Scots hinders
yer progress in society! I prefer tae think alang the lines o the auld
Scots saw . . . 'Thaim wi a guid Scots tongue in their heid are fit tae
gang ower the warld!'

Nou ae story like that, guid tho it is duisnae create a tradeition
— no every customs offeicial can reel aff stanzas fae Burns, but
Scotland is gey unique in haein sic a strang workin cless intellectual
tradeition. A frien o mine the poet Ellie McDonald wes debatin
this point — maybe it verged on flytin — on the train hame tae
Dundee efter a poetry festival in Edinburgh. The English poet she
wes sittin aside admitted that the Burns tradeition wes widespread
but fowk like her exaggerated and romanticised it — an it certainly
didnae gae faurer nor quotin a pickle weel kennt lines. Confident,

the poet jaloused he wad test his theory, sae when the guard came alang the train tae check the tickets, he spiered at him gin he kennt ony Scottish poetry. The guard reponed that he kennt his Burns richt eneuch, but that his favourite lines were fae anither poet....

Ae weet forenicht i' the yow-trummle
I saw yon antrin thing,
A watergaw wi its chitterin licht
Ayont the on-ding;
An I thocht o the last wild look ye gied
Afore ye deed

There was nae reek i' the laverock's hoose
that nicht - an nane i' mine;
But I hae thocht o that foolish licht
Ever sinsyne;
an I think that mebe at last I ken
What your look meant then.

The guard had been a communist activist in his younger days, an had imbibed the socialist an nationalist ideals o MacDiarmid. Noo I like tae think positively, but I'm no shuir how monie stories like that will be tellt in the future, hoo much langer we can coorie in tae the douce bield o the culture an ignore its erosion aw about us.

The flicht intae sang an culture at the expense o politics is no as easily tenable as it aince wes. Because at ae time aw Scots were cultural nationalists — even if yer expression o it wes wavin the saltire at a fitba match — it wes there in the bluid, a gut feeling a kennin wha ye were an where ye cam frae. But mair an mair I fear folk's ruits in the culture are weakenin. The groundbase of the culture has cheingit dramatically in recent years — whiles I jalouse that some sowels — and theres a wheen o them about —get buskit in their braws an celebrate their sense of Scottishness as a flicht frae reality, a wee holiday frae the workaday world — a couthy interlude afore getting back to business. In Lewis Grassic Gibbons

Sunset Song — it wes the English side o us that had nae depth, nae roots:

> So that was Chris and her reading and schooling, two Chrisses there were that fought for her heart and tormented her. You hated the land and the coarse speak of the folk and learning was brave and fine one day and the next you'd waken with the peewits crying across the hills, deep and deep, crying in the heart of you and the smell of the earth in your face, almost you'd cry for that, the beauty of it and the sweetness of the Scottish land and skies. You saw their faces in firelight, father's and mother's and the neighbours, before the lamps lit up, tired and kind, faces dear and close to you, you wanted the words they'd known and used, forgotten in the far-off youngness of their lives, Scots words to tell to your heart how they wrung it and held it, the toil of their days and unendingly their fight. And the next minute that passed from you, you were English, back to the English words so sharp and clean and true — for a while, for a while, till they slid so smooth from your throat you knew they could never say anything that was worth the saying at all.

Now, I'm gey feart that for monie o us it is the Scottish side. The strength of Scottish culture aye lay in the uncompromising Scottishness o the mass o the population — the aristocracy, with a few notable exceptions have been on permanent holiday from Scottish culture since the Union — a strain of fowk that hes gaed agley, living in the country but not of it. By gaein that gait, they became an irrelevance to Scottish culture, an they could blithely stey an irrelevance as lang as thay strang bonds atween writers and people remained, and the people remained whit they aye were — Scots and nothing but Scots. A guid example is the minin population o Scotland.

Baith my gran-faithers wes miners, ane o thaim had a semi nomadic existence sinkin pits in Sooth Africa, Ayrshire, the Lothians an Fife. Yet he had a strang sense o belangin— a sense that miners an their faimilies were the core o the nation — an he wes richt for at ae time it wes reckoned that they made up a fifth o the population o Scotland. They developed a communal culture, but were often regardit as a caste apairt by the rest o the folk — in East Fife for example the fisher fowk cried the denizens o the miners raws 'the aff scoorins o Scotland'. I'm workin on a television history o the Scots miners the nou, an their history is nothin for the country tae be prood o. In Andra Fletcher's day they an their bairns wes bound til a maister like slaves. There's nae danger therefore o miners, or me, fawin intae the trap o nostalgia for the pure never-never land o the guid auld days. Scotland wes simply whit wrocht them, an guid or bad, they were prood o belangin — prood o the fact that they were the core o the nation — Scots and nothing else but Scots in speech an culture — aye, an especially in the songs they sang.

They wad hae agreed wi Fletcher: Ken yer ballads, yer sangs, yer poetry an it duisnae maitter a haet wha maks the laws. Ye're secure in yer culture — ye dinna need tae shout aboot it when ye've got it. The masses had it — MacDiarmid said the core o ocht is only for the few — he wes wrang — here the core was the mass o folk who couldnae be ocht else but Scots. An like maist guid things it wesnae exclusive. I mind fower year syne daein an interview wi an auld Spanish gentleman that steyed in Logan in Ayrshire — ane o the last o the first generation that had come ower tae wark in the iron works at Lugar, syne the pits o sooth Ayrshire. He an I naturally spoke Ayrshire Scots wi ane anither, but when the tape recorder wes switched on he did that very Scottish thing o tryin tae speak in standard English, literally translatin and transformin himsel for the new situation. The skeelie fluency o his Scots wes replaced by stilted, hesitant English. I wes aboot tae stop the tape tae see if I could get him back tae his ain wey o speakin, when his wife who wes also born in Andalucia but brocht up in Ayrshire, interrupted him an said "Hey you, stop pittin it on . . . talk Scots like the rest o us!"

Ane o the factors that created sic a strang sense o belangin for thaim wes their ideal o helpin ane anither — they couldnae no help ane anither, it wes ingrained in them as pairt o their Scottishness. A story cam doon tae me through my faimily that gaes back tae

Goston at the time o the 1921 Lock Oot. The Kays leived in a Miners' Raw cried Manse Close ahint the Auld Parish Kirk in the centre o the toun. Durin the strike a boy fae the neebourin faimily, the McSkimmings veisited an aulder brither o his that wrocht in Ayr. Haein a wage, the brither insisted on giein the boy a pound tae help oot the faimily at hame, but the boy had been tellt by his parents tae refuse for they kennt the brither needed his wages for his ain immediate faimily tae survive. The brither didnae press the issue but gied his younger brither an auld coat tae tak hame for his ain use. On the bus hame, though, he found that his brither had secreted the pound fauldit up in the inside pooch o the coat. Noo a pound wes a lot o money in that place at that time an wad hae gaen a lang wey tae help that ane faimily o McSkimmings survive, but whit the boy did when the bus reached Goston Cross was tae gae intae the café an buy 40 fish suppers — ane for every man, woman an wean in Manse Close.

An if folk didnae agree wi that wey o luikin at the warld, there wes bother. This is Tam, fae Willie McIlvanney's fine novel *Docherty* tellin his boy why he shouldnae contract for the coal owners.

Son, it's easy tae be gud oan a fu' belly. It's when a man's goat two bites an' wan o' them he'll share, ye ken whit he's made o'. Maist o' them were boarn blin'. Well, we areny, son. We canny afford to be blin'. Listen. In any country in the world, who are the only folk that ken whit it's like tae leeve in that country? The folk at the boattom. The rest can a' kid themselves oan. They can afford to hiv fancy ideas. We canny, son. We loass the wan idea o' who we are, we're deid. We're wan anither. Tae survive, we'll respect wan anither. When the time comes, we'll a' move forward thegither, or nut at all. That's whit Ah've goat against you, boay.' He pointed at Angus. 'You're a fuckin' deserter. Ah don't harbour deserters. Ye're wi' the rest o' us or ye go elsebit'

These people were classified recently by the Government as the Enemy Within — not because of the confrontations on the picket lines — but because they hold values of a communal nature which are anathema to the Mind Thy Self morality of those in power in the British state today. We micht no aw be miners, but I hope I'm richt in thinkin that maist Scots still care aboot whit happens tae thaim thats no sae weel aff, an resent the increasin imposition o alien values.

We were weel warned o it by Fletcher of Saltoun:

> those who have contrived schemes of constitutions, have, as I think always framed them with respect only to particular nations, for whom they were designed, and without any regard to the rest of mankind. Since as they could not but know that every society, as well as every private man, has a natural inclination to exceed in everything, and draw all advantages to itself, they might also have seen the necessity of curbing that exorbitant inclination, and obliging them to consider the general good and interest of mankind, on which that of every distinct society does in a great measure depend. And one would think that politicians, who ought to be the best of all moral philosophers, should have considered what a citizen of the world is.

Maybe we could afford to be apolitical in the past when the culture and the values contained in it were solid. Nou, it's aw under attack, and the signs o the attack are aw roun about us — Poll Tax, which taks the same fae rich an puir; schuil boards which will tak money out of educational facilities and be uised tae undermine the schuil in the hope it will opt out and become a fee-paying élitist establishment, again for the well-to-do; scunnersome politicians comin north an condescendingly addressing the Scots as if we were recalcitrant crabbit bairns, telling us no tae hae a dependancy culture, yet daein nocht about our unrequited desire for mair independence!

As the contemporary ballad makars, the Proclaimers, say in a recent sang, 'What do you when democracy dies?'

Some have already gien up through brain washing, and I obtain perverse enjoyment collecting examples o the Scottish Cringe at its worst .... an education spokesman in a regional authority recently rejecting a motion that Scottish culture be gien due pride of place in the schools curriculum by saying that we live in a multi-cultural environment! Scottish culture is not to be one of the multis taught apparently. This is part of the anti-parochial fixation of much of the left — our visionary internationalists who seem to be blinded by the whiteness of the cliffs of Dover — sae thirled to the culture of Little England they are. Anither example fae personal experience . . . a Fife heidmaister dismissin the lack of Scottish studies taught in his primary schuil wi the words, 'Oh, this is not a very Scottish area!'

Baith are products of the centuries of cultural colonialism, that again, Fletcher foretellt:

> All our affairs since the union of the crowns have been managed by the advice of English ministers, and the principle offices of the kingdom, filled with such men, as the court of England knew would be subservient to their designs: by which means they have had so visible an influence upon our whole administration, that we have from that time appeared to the rest of the world more like a conquered province than a free independent people.

An it got a lot waur efter the incorporating Union!

Nou I'm aware o the death wish the establishment has aye wished on the culture, an the last thing I want tae dae is mak statements which support the death wish — because the death wish has usually got it wrang — for example, the literati telling Burns no tae fash himsel writing in Scots for naebody wad understaun it in the neist generation. Here we are twa hunder year on, speaking it an I hope, understaunin it. That wes wishful thinkin by the establishment an it has aye been wishful thinkin — because for the mass a folk, the Scotchness couldna be dirled oot o them through education — ye juist adapted for the meenits ye comunicated wi the teacher, then gaed back tae Scots, tae bein yersel. But great minds hae been taen in by the deathwish. This is Lewis Grassic Gibbon and his his eloquent epitaph for "the last of the old Scots folk" at the end of the novel Sunset Song:

A new generation comes up that will know them not, except as a
memory in a song, they passed with the things that seemed good to
them with loves and desires that grow dim and alien in the days to
be. It was the old Scotland that perished then, and we may believe
that never again will the old speech and the old songs, the old curses
and the old benedictions rise but with alien effort to their lips.

They may hae thocht it wes happennin in their lifetimes, but in
retrospect, they were juist prophesyin whit in fact is happenin in
oor ain — an wi a speed unimaginable in Gibbon's day. For Gibbon
wes tae dee afore mass communications, especially television bit
intae the culture.

My generation, born and brocht up in the '50s is the last o the
pre-tv generations, and because of that our cultural attitudes are
rooted in a stronger sense of place — the Scottish village, if you
like, rather than that global village which in fact reflects a gey
narrow angle on urban Anglo-American society. Although we were
pre-tv, we were a lang wey fae being the last of the peasants
eulogised by Gibbon. Our culture was American music and movies,
and Scottish music and poetry in equal measure — in a faimily sing-
song Rabbie and Elvis wad be gien equal laldy! In the praisent
though, there's nae contest — the Anglo-American side wins hands
doun.

Dinnae bother aboot the laws, gin ye can compose the sangs —
but whit happens gin ye canna sing the sangs, canna even
understaun the meanin o the words, an get nuthin in your education
to encourage you to attempt to understaun, tae sing even 'with alien
effort'?

Sae whit dae we dae? Dae we accept that the prophecies, that
the death wish has finally borne bitter fruit, and assimilate, become
de-racinated *assimilados*, wha accept the culture o their colonial
overlords?

No! The human loss is ower ill tae thole, the culture too rich to
consign to the academics, the sangs faur too braw tae sing wi alien
effort — they hae tae be sung wi the hert, an mind and soul, but

maistly wi the hert, for it's there we ken oorsels maist o aw. There, we ken that tae be onythin else but Scots, is tae lea tae oorsels and the fowk we stem frae.

Naw, we keep the faith o women and men like Fletcher. We chip awa at the fause monolith till it comes doun, howk oot the gowden seam o oor ain culture — no because it's better or waur nor ony ither culture, but juist because it's oors an the core o ocht that we are, o ocht worth bein. Fletcher wes deaved that when we lost the parliament, in the long run there wad be nocht o the culture left. 'Ye cannae dae ocht gin ye've nocht tae dae ocht wi' as the sayin goes. We've tholed as a nation by singin the sangs, but for the sangs tae be sung in the future, we hiv tae gae back tae the fundaments o Fletchers original belief — that a people needs a parliament tae represent it — an I promise ye when that day comes, as come it will for aw that, by here, ye'll hear some singin.

I dedicate this tae the glorious memory o Andra Fletcher a' Saltoun, Scotsman and Patriot.

1989

The Union: a Terrible Mistake

David Simpson

David Simpson was Economic Adviser to the Standard
Life Assurance Company from 1988 to 2001. He was
previously Professor of Economics at Strathclyde
University. He contested the parliamentary seat of
Berwick and East Lothian for the SNP in 1970 and in
February 1974.

The Union: a Terrible Mistake

David Simpson

It is a privilege to have been invited by the Saltire Society to speak at this occasion honouring Andrew Fletcher of Saltoun, who lies buried in the vaults beneath us.

Those who have spoken in previous years include such distinguished scholars as Geoffrey Barrow, Paul Scott, Elizabeth Whitley, David Daiches and Gordon Donaldson. When I was invited to be this year's speaker, I was at once aware that I had little to say which could measure up to the standard of their contributions.

At the same time, I felt that I could not refuse an invitation to speak in this Kirk, where my father was for many years the Session Clerk. The village and parish of Saltoun have many happy memories for me, but my principal reason for deciding to accept is because I was fortunate enough to he present at some of the early ceremonies begun, I think in the late l960s, by David and Margaret Mill Irving. Although the plaque had been placed on the outside wall by the Saltire Society in 1955, it was the Mill Irvings who began these Annual Commemorations, and who invited to their home afterwards for tea the small number who in those days attended.

I am sure that all of us who remember those occasions do so with great respect and affection for David and Margaret Mill Irving and for what they did. We must also be grateful to the Saltire Society for carrying the standard which the Mill Irvings raised.

Having, for these reasons, decided to accept the invitation to speak here today, I was left with the problem of finding something to say. There is nothing about Fletcher and his times which I could add to the contributions of the distinguished historians I have mentioned. I therefore decided it must be on a contemporary theme, but you will be relieved to hear that my remarks will not be about economics. They will be about politics.

Although the Saltire Society is not a political organisation, I do not feel that I should apologise for addressing a contemporary political issue, since Fletcher's reputation rests as much on his writings on the political events of his own time as upon his political activities. The political question which I should like to address is this: Why is it that so few people in Scotland— to those of us who share Fletcher's views, a painfully small number — desire the independence of their country? The overwhelming majority of the Scottish people still support the political union with England, a union which no man or woman strove harder than Andrew Fletcher to try to prevent. When he had failed in this purpose, he left Scotland and spent the remainder of his life in self-imposed exile, first in London, later in Paris. His parting words about this country are reputed to be that it was 'fit only for the slaves that sold it'.

It is easy for contemporary nationalists, looking back to the Union of 1707, to persuade themselves that the majority in the Scottish Parliament who voted in favour of the Union were either rogues or fools, or both. In the words of one of Burns' songs, they were 'bought and sold for English gold.' It is certainly true that the Scots Parliament of 1707 was not representative, by modern standards, of the whole population. But as the proportion of the population entitled to vote has grown, there has not, at least until quite recently, been any corresponding growth in opposition to the Union. The uncomfortable fact is that for the last two hundred years or so, the Union has been tacitly accepted by the great majority of the people, although the anniversaries of the Union have never been occasions for celebration, not even on the part of Unionists themselves. Even today the only political party which is opposed to the Union has never gained more than 30% of the vote at nationwide elections. Why should this be? It is not good enough to say that the majority are simply misled by the Unionists. The reasons why people vote for unionist parties deserve serious examination.

I believe that there are two main reasons why people vote unionist. First, there is the belief that a voter's interests are best served if he puts his class interests above his national interests. The passionate hositility of many middle class people to independence or to any form of devolution can be traced fairly easily to what may be described as a fear of socialism or communism or a fear of the working class.

This point of view was most succinctly expressed a few years ago by a leading middle-class member of the Labour Party in Scotland, when he said that he would rather live under a Conservative Government in the UK than under a Labour Government in an independent Scotland. (Since 1979, he got his wish, and to his credit, he has publicly regretted it). This remark echoes an equally notorious saying which has often been used to illustrate the atmosphere of defeatism which played such a large part in the fall of France in 1940, in the War which began fifty years ago tomorrow. It was said of many of the French middle class of the 1930s that they preferred Hitler to Leon Blum. This is an attitude which is as difficult for a nationalist to understand as is the passionate dislike shown by some contemporary Scottish businessmen towards Donald Dewar.

It was also said of France in 1940 that many of the more politically active members of the working class felt that their interests were likely to be better served by the Soviet Union than by their own countrymen of a different social class.

This habit of putting class interests (real or imagined) above national interests has been just as disastrous for Scotland as it was for France, although less dramatic. Let us call it the Vichy tendency, after the Government which ruled occupied France from July 1940 to August 1944.

It has been convenient for the victors of World War II — above all the Free French — to pretend that the Vichy government was no more than a tiny handful of right-wing fanatics who were thrust on an unwilling population by the Germans. Nothing could be further from the truth. Marshal Petain was elected Prime Minister by an overwhelming vote of the French National Assembly, and he was later entrusted with unlimited powers by an even larger majority.

It is easy for all of us to identify with the wartime French Resistance to Vichy and to Hitler, and to say 'This is what I should have done.' The sad truth is that in parallel situations, we are far more likely to act like the majority of the French population who supported Vichy. Charles de Gaulle showed that there are times when to save a nation's deepest values one must disobey the State — even when that State is apparently legitimised by majority voting. France after 1940 was one of those times.

In drawing parallels between contemporary Scotland and Vichy France, it is tempting to indulge in a search for correspondences among the leading characters on the political stage. It is not difficult to find in Scotland the counterpart of Marshal Pétain, an old man of patriotic reputation and experienced statesmanship. But when the moment of choice came, he put the interests of party before the needs of his country.

Nor is it difficult to find a Scottish politician to correspond to Pierre Laval — a career politician who, realising that the source of political power lay outside the country, would do anything which that power asked him to do in order to further his career. France in the early 1940s swarmed with fanatics from the radical right who enjoyed the security of German embassy pensions and a cardboard world of fictitious power.

The political lesson which we can draw today from the experience of such men is the following: each sought to establish their credentials with Hitler, the man from whom flowed all political power at that time in France, by trying to prove to him how ideologically sound they were. What they did not realise was that Hitler was not interested in ideology — he was really only interested in establishing German domination over Europe in general, and France in particular. For Hitler, ideology was no more than a means to this end.

I said a few moments ago that I thought there were two strands of thought or feeling underlying the Unionist view. The first, the placing of class above national interest, I have called the Vichy tendency. The second may be called economic self-interest.

Adam Smith, David Hume and the other members of the 18th century Enlightenment in Scotland were certainly neither fools nor rogues. Nor did they question the benefits of the Union to Scotland. They regarded such of their contemporaries as were hostile to the Union, mainly Jacobites, as romantics, backward-looking and irrational. They felt themselves on the other hand, to be cosmopolitan. The Union therefore seemed to them to be a step in the direction of Progress. By giving up its sovereignty in the interests of the wider good, Scotland was setting an example for the rest of the world to follow.

In this respect, as in many others, their expectations were disappointed. No other European country followed the Scottish example of voluntarily allowing itself to be incorporated in another nation.

In one respect, however, their expectation about the Union was satisfied. Scotland's access to the markets of England and the Empire did allow her to prosper, even if her gains were much smaller than those of England, and even if other comparable European countries prospered without such access.

Today, however, Scottish economic prosperity is no longer conditional on access to the single market of the UK or of the Empire (the latter has ceased to exist); it depends to an increasing extent on what happens in the future single market of the European Community. And what happens in that market is heavily influenced by political decisions which will more and more be taken in Brussels, not London.

That being the case, the logic of the Unionist argument that Scotland's economic interests within the single market of the United Kingdom are best served by representation at the top political table, that is, by having a seat in the Cabinet, leads inevitably to the conclusion that within the single market of the European Community Scotland must have membership of the

Council of Ministers as a sovereign nation. This is the counterpart of a seat in the Cabinet. The opposite argument, namely that Scotland would have more influence as part of a single UK representation implies that Scotland would be better represented in the UK Cabinet not by its own Secretary of State but by other Ministers.

The need for political representation at the topmost table (a Unionist argument) is reinforced by the fact that the role of government in everyday life has changed beyond recognition since the 18th century. Most people in 18th century Scotland would go through their lives without encountering any of the institutions of Government, since at that time the functions of government were largely restricted to Defence, Justice and External Affairs. Consequently, the Union of 1707 made little difference to the ordinary lives of most Scottish people. They simply did not encounter Government or its representatives.

Today, however, there is scarcely any part of a citizen's life which is not touched by political decisions, above all on such central issues as Health, Education and Social Security. It is therefore even more important today than it was in Fletcher's time that Scottish political interests should be properly represented.

It would be foolish for me to pretend that I am primarily moved by such logical appeals to economic interest. Like Andrew Fletcher, I believe that the Union with England was a terrible mistake, just as the Vichy regime was a terrible mistake for France, and that the Union with England would still have been a terrible mistake, even if Scotland had become as a result a more populous and a more prosperous country than it is today.

Both the Union and the Vichy regime came into existence in ways entirely consistent with the constitutional procedures which prevailed in their respective times and places. Both therefore had a legal legitimacy, but neither has ever enjoyed what may be called, for want of a better phrase, a moral legitimacy.

Let us hope that whoever performs the task of re-opening the Scottish Parliament will share something of the moral and historical sensitivity felt by Charles de Gaulle. Standing on the steps of the Hotel de Ville at the moment of the Liberation of Paris, he was invited by General Catroux to declare the Restoration of the Third Republic, which had been formally abolished when the Vichy regime came to power. De Gaulle replied that he could not do this, because the Republic had never ceased to exist. With this remark, he consigned the whole shameful episode of Vichy to the waste paper basket of history.

1990

The Age of Nationalism

Arnold Kemp

Arnold Kemp was Deputy Editor of *The Scotsman* for nine years until 1981 when he took over as Editor of *The Herald*, remaining there until 1994. He continued to write on Scottish topics for the *Observer* until his untimely death in 2002. He is the son of the celebrated Scottish playwright Robert Kemp and his publications include *The Hollow Drum* (1993).

The Age of Nationalism

Arnold Kemp

It is a great honour to have been invited to give this address in memory of Andrew Fletcher of Saltoun. I am also very happy that Paul Scott should be here today. Paul has more or less completed a new book on Fletcher of Saltoun. It is to be published by Edinburgh University Press next year. I am indebted to his earlier work— *1707: The Union of Scotland and England* — for the quotation with which I begin today. It is from Fletcher's *State of the Controversy betwixt United and Separate Parliaments* (1706):

> The Scots deserve no pity, if they voluntarily surrender their united and separate interests to the mercy of an united Parliament, where the English shall have so vast a majority.

This is the age of nationalism. It has proved to be a much more resilient vehicle than communism. In his new book about de Gaulle, Regis Debray discusses the nature of nationalism, and distinguishes between ethnic and elective nationalism.

The first arises because of the homogeneity of a people. The second is a solution to the opposite condition: peoples of different origins may choose a common nationalism because they have to invent workable institutions and instruments.

Elective nationalism is found in its most obvious form in the United States, which is a melting pot of races. Despite its evident racial tensions the US has achieved genuine national coherence.

Scottish nationalism arises from the concepts of ethnic nationalism, but can it survive in this form in the latter part of the twentieth century? Inexorable and irreversible changes are affecting the character of

Scotland, as indeed they are of all comparable parts of the world.

Racial tensions in England reflect the difficulties of moving from concepts of ethnic nationalism, based on racial homogeneity, towards a new reality of elective nationalism supported by a multiracial society.

Ethnic nationalism is at work in Eastern Europe after a long period of oppression but its face can be ugly. This is shown in the persecution of one national group by another, in Romania for example. Nor can it ever be forgotten that Nazism fed on ethnic nationalism of an extreme and unpleasant kind.

This year I had the good fortune to visit both Estonia and Georgia and as a Scot was extremely interested in their struggle to be free of the political embrace of a large neighbour. The histories of the two countries are somewhat different. Apart from a relatively brief period before the war, Estonia has always been a pawn in the affairs of the great powers. It fell into the Russia sphere after the infamous Ribbentrop-Molotov pact. Since the war the Russians have implanted substantial numbers of their own nationals. This has considerably complicated the Estonian drive to independence, which has gained in assertiveness since the beginning of perestroika six years ago. The presence in the country of large numbers of Russians who have no desire to leave makes comparisons with Northern Ireland inescapable.

By contrast, Georgia, in the nineteenth century, joined itself to Russia, became a Russian protectorate, to form a Christian bastion against Islam. Russia dominated Georgia in much the same way England has dominated Scotland. Georgia had a brief period of independence after the First World War but this was snuffed out in 1921 by the triumph of the Bolsheviks. Of course, Georgia gave Stalin to the world.

Both countries have resisted cultural assimilation very largely, it seems to me, because each has its own language. Although Estonians and Georgians have all been obliged to learn Russian, Estonian and Georgian remain incomprehensible to most Russians. This has given the smaller nations a considerable psychological advantage. In Ireland, of course, the language question was an important focus for the nationalist movement in its early days. But threequarters of a century of state patronage has not really slowed the decline of the Irish language. Without comparable sponsorship, our own Gaelic has shown as much, if not more, residual vigour. But because Ireland has established its own independence and is comfortable with it, it can be more relaxed about the assimilative cultural forces to which it, as a largely English speaking country, is open almost as much as Scotland.

Scotland has few means of resisting these forces. Most of our important institutions have been anglicised since the war. Chief among these have been the universities, which are organised on a UK basis. You will remember that our universities were among the leading opponents of devolution in the seventies. In a country with a scientific and intellectual tradition such as ours this was a bitter pill for many of us to swallow.

Paul Scott has campaigned vigorously for a Scottish national theatre. I am, I have to confess, suspicious of any proposal that would set up yet another arts bureaucracy. We have had some very unpalatable examples in Glasgow this year of how ruthless the arts bureaucracy can be in its pursuit of power and patronage. I do share Paul's distress that, with the very honourable exception of the smaller companies like Borderline and Wildcat, there are so few vehicles for indigenous Scottish actors and dramatists.

Again the comparison with Ireland is humbling. As Dublin prepares to don the mantle of European City of Culture in 1991, it can refect that its theatre, a rich tradition, is in great shape. The Gate company — ironically not the national theatre, which is the Abbey — is outstanding by any yardstick. In Brian Friel, Ireland has one of the outstanding contemporary playwrights.

My father was chairman of the Edinburgh Gateway Company after the war and was part of the movement, of which Bridie was the father figure, to establish a distinctive Scottish theatrical tradition. Their argument was that the existence of *The Three Estates* proved that one had existed before the departure of the Court with the Union of the Crowns but that this tradition had been killed by subsequent lack of patronage. This theatrical winter was of course made much more severe by the dominance of the presbyterian tradition.

That Scots law has become something of a backwater was the theme of an article in the *Herald* the other day by Lord McCluskey. He warned that it was in danger of being excluded from the development of European law. The idea that because it was in its roots more similar to the European tradition gave it some sort of advantage was, he said, a fairy tale. On the criminal side Scots law has indeed influenced English practice but it seems to have become a machine for putting people in jail and recent scandals in the judiciary suggested that this protected and sheltered elite had surrendered to some kind of complacency.

Indeed, the Kirk's dominance of our national life began to wane with the Disruption, when it was lured into a contest with the temporal powers which it could not win. The contrast in the twentieth century with Ireland is again interesting. De Valera, in his drive to consolidate independence, appointed the Catholic church to a position of national guardianship. The result was indeed a consolidated independence. But there was a heavy price to be paid in the form of an oppressive literary censorship. In Scotland we live in a secular age and the church's influence is feeble. It no longer attracts so many people of the first intellectual rank to make a career in it — that is not to say there are no able people in the Kirk.

A balance sheet of sorts begins to emerge. The price of close union with England is cultural assimilation and dominance. The Scottish economy, on the edge of Europe, has to be an open economy. So too must be its culture. On the other hand closing the door to external influence is a recipe for stagnation and mediocrity. That is the dilemma faced by modern Scotland,

These forces all make it difficult for us to develop a convincing ethnic nationalism. Apart from the new Scots (who may still perceive themselves as English or British though some become more

Scottish than the Scots), we cannot cut ourselves off from the wider polity and economy. The balkanisation of the UK would be a nightmare.

This difficulty is made worse by the fact that, even without its new population, Scotland is itself culturally diverse. We are not one country with a dominant metropolis. We are a very curious country — our real capital city, London, is not within our own boundaries. We have four cites with extensive hinterlands, each with their own strong personalities, and caught up in rivalry with each other. We have vast, thinly populated rural regions which are deeply suspicious of the central belt.

During the devolution referendum in the seventies, these differences were skilfully exploited by the opponents of change, and indeed they explain why Scotland has found it difficult to combine politically. The Republic of Ireland is highly centralised, with its economy and political system based on Dublin: it would be impossible, and indeed dangerous, to replicate such a system in Scotland. If Scotland were to win its independence within the European Community then its own constitution would have to reflect its personality and balance its regional interests. Without such safeguards Scotland would quickly fall apart.

Since the war, of course, there have been forces hostile to bourgeois theatre, which was the genre in which my father and most of his contemporaries worked. It fell out of fashion. Rattigan was supplanted by Osborne. Brecht's influence began to be felt everywhere. The repertory theatres in Glasgow, Edinburgh, Dundee and Perth were municipalised and largely became part of a UK circuit under the patronage of the Arts Council. All suffered a loss of Scottish identity to a greater or lesser degree. Indeed the historian of the Citizens, Michael Coveney, remarks in his new book that the Citz not only reject the Scottish tradition, they rejected the English one too and tried to work within a European framework.

I wish the Citz nothing but good. They have done great service for the cause of theatre in Glasgow and Scotland, reviving a habit a theatre-going which seemed on the point of death. But the essential work of the theatre — of reflecting and lampooning our own culture — has too often gone by default in the major venues. It was carried on by such companies as 7:84, Wildcat and Borderline. Although they all enjoyed official patronage of one kind or another, they became a kind of alternative theatre.

It was no accident that they found most of their inspiration in Scotland's socialist tradition. Scottish working-class culture has proved suprisingly robust. It is the mainspring both of modern Scottish writing and drama. By contrast the bourgeois tradition has grown feeble because it has been more open to anglicisation. The middle classes have been heavily exposed to assimilative processes. In the last couple of decades many people have come to Scotland from the south. They work in the new industries or penetrate the professions, or are part of growing population of rentiers and second-home owners.

Such people may be seeking an enhanced quality of life; they may be making a career move into what they perceive as a provincial arena in the hope of distinguishing themselves in it and returning to London eventually; they may be retiring on investments gathered from a commercial or professional life in the much richer south. Whatever their motives, many of there make a genuine commitment to Scotland. Their presence among us is a fact of life and is often an adornment of it. Indeed, if you go to comparable non-metropolitan regions of Europe or the US, you will observe that exactly the same tendencies are taking place. One thinks of Aquitaine in France, where the holiday homes begin to outnumber those of the natives, or Connecticut in the US where the rich refugees from New York co-exist with the local red-necks.

Even the institutions guaranteed by the Union, the church and the law, are in various kinds of difficulty. The protection of Scots law has made it largely resistant to English infiltration. But this is not in every way beneficial. It has protected our criminal tradition but it has sidelined mercantile law. For example, the suppliers of the *Glasgow Herald's* new presses insisted that the contract be written in English law. There seems a danger that Scots law will be driven into a rather squalid ghetto of criminal practice, trust work, domestic law and conveyancing. It comes as no surprise to be told that London is also the point at which Britain's European legal expertise is developing.

There interesting differences between our historical experience and that of small countries like Georgia, Estonia arid Ireland. Chief among those is the fact that Scotland has not been oppressed. Oppression is perhaps an essential precondition for active nationalism, England's attitude to Scotland has been benign if sometimes patronising or arrogant. It has left Scotland to its own devices and has accepted the need to equalise the resources available for public services.

This means that public expenditure in Scotland exceeds the amount raised by taxation in Scotland. Generations of Scots civil servants have quietly achieved this result by their patient and subtle diplomacy in Whitehall. The late Sir Douglas Haddow, the chief civil servant in Scotland during the seventies, was opposed to devolution because he knew he could achieve more for Scotland within the machinery of Whitehall. By an irony, it was the devolution debate in the seventies which awakened England to Scotland's apparent advantage. This new awareness explains some of the English resentment that came to the fore this year during the debate on the closure of Ravenscraig, and the outburst in the *Evening Standard* and the *Economist*.

This so-called advantage needs some qualification, because the higher figures of public spending per head in Scotland do not reveal the enormous concentrations of wealth in England, which remains a much richer country. The figures arise partly from the higher proportion of public housing in Scotland. They also reflect the higher unit cost of delivering public services to a country with one of the lowest population densities in Europe. England's wealth is rooted in its property and its invested wealth, and the Thatcher regime discriminates heartily in favour of the property-owner through mortgage relief. Scotland was also more highly taxed than

England through the rating system, and it has been amusing to hear the English outrage as this anomoly has been corrected through the introduction of the poll tax. .

Even if much of the English criticism is simplistic, it's an ill wind — for among some of the excessive and indeed abusive statements are more sensible reflections. Among these is the observation that the Tories root-and-branch opposition to devolution has distorted political life in Scotland. Mrs Thatcher has bound us together to a remarkable degree. Labour's dominance is artificial in that it arises from a genuine Scottish dislike of the values of Thatcherism rather than a universal commitment to socialist principles.

Indeed. Labour's dominance is somewhat exaggerated since it has only one MP north of the Highland line. The dislike of Thatcherism is because it is inimical to certain Scottish interests. But it also has an emotional component which seems to affect all classes and sometimes surpasses all reasonable explanation. It's as if the people of Scotland have discerned the fact that they are regarded at the highest levels of this Government with a disdain amounting to contempt. With the departure of Mr Michael Forsyth from the chairmanship of the party in Scotland, is it foolish to believe that the party may now be persuaded to join the devolutionary consensus?

The unpopularity of the Conservatives does not just arise from the popular perception that they are now an anti-Scottish party. There are grievances that are real and specific. Some of our great assets— our universities, our teaching hospitals — are perceived as liabilities and attacked. On the contrary they clearly have an economic value since they provide a service in great and growing demand — it is the way they are financed that causes endless dificulties. Indeed they must form the basis of our future economic prosperity for this must depend on high value intellectual-based services and industries. Our scientific and intellectual community must not be eroded. Our medical excellence is a precious resource since health care too is a growth industry in which Scotland by dint of its native tradition has a leading position.

If that is a bourgeois grievance, then the decline of our heavy industries bears disproportionately on our working classes. Like Cobbett's agrarian labourers, they are paying for the prosperity of what he called the Dead Weight, the rentiers, the speculators, the public servants. The price is paid in the form of long term unemployment, resentment, pessimism and emigration.

The case for Scottish independence within the European Community would have to be justified by the perception that Scottish interests are genuinely different from those of England and that a Scottish Parliament could express them and safeguard them more effectively. It is ironic that we owe to an English backlash the fact that Scottish independence is, for the first time, truly on the political agenda.

If it were negotiated with goodwill, and within the constitutional, political and economic framework of the European Community which removes the prospect of separatism and exclusion, then we have nothing to fear from it. Indeed the development of federal relationships within the United Kingdom has long been the best hope of modernising the Union.

What we are hearing from the south, in increasingly strident tones, are the first cries of distress as the Westminster Parliament begins to sense its own supremacy under threat. The European reality is beginning to be felt at every level and is indeed working as a compensating force against the indifference of the Thatcher Government to such questions as public health and safety and minimum guarantees for employees. If genuine political union does not develop in Europe, then the Council of Ministers, subject to sovereign national Parliaments, must in time be superseded by federal European institutions.

After the devolution fiasco in the seventies, I despaired of ever seeing a Scottish Parliament in my lifetime. I am now more hopeful than I have ever been that it is coming before too long. My vision is not that of the romantic nationalist: the well-being of the people of Scotland must be an important constraint on the wilder impulses of constitutional visionaries. But Scotland is not alone in Europe as a small nation which feels emotionally frustrated. The European spirit is genuine and the small forgotten nations now perceive that they may find their place in the sun— without the evils of balkanisation.

The idea of Scottishness cannot be based on romantic historic concepts. In the definition of Regis Debray Scottish nationalism must be elective because it is reasonable, and conforms to the reality of modern Scotland. Anything else would be romantic tosh. But it would be odd if the new punitive spirit of some English commentators, who would cut us off without a penny, were to produce a new bloom in a forgotten garden, for an oppressed or insulted nation will put the recovery of its dignity beyond the realms of petty economic calculation.

1991

On Patriotism

William Ferguson

William Ferguson was Reader in Scottish History, at the University of Edinburgh until 1989. His publications include: *Scotland 1639 to the Present* (volume 4 of the Edinburgh History of Scotland, 1968), *Scotland's Relations with England* (1977 and 1994) and *The Identity of the Scottish Nation* (1998) which won the Saltire Award as historical publication of the year.

On Patriotism

William Ferguson

We are here today to commemorate Andrew Fletcher, laird of Saltoun, who was born in 1653 and died in 1716. He was a great Scot, one of the finest his country has ever produced; and I venture to think that he was also a truly great man.

One curious feature of this annual commemoration needs to be explained at the outset. Usually we commemorate people deemed worthy of remembrance on the anniversary of their birthdays. Thus we all know whose day the 25th of January is, though most of us would be hard pushed to recall that Robert Burns died on the 21st day of July. We meet today, however, to mark the death of Andrew Fletcher, who died in London on 15th September 1716. There is a simple reason for that curious reversal of the usual practice: we don't know Fletcher's date of birth, though the year was certainly 1653. Indeed, much of his life is obscured by lack of documentation arising from the somewhat mysterious loss of his papers in the mid 18th century.

But we know enough about him to be sure that he was a man, not just of his time, but for all time. There is, indeed, a timeless quality about Andrew Fletcher. If that 'man for all seasons' were with us today he would find familiar challenges to his remarkable powers of political insight and incisive comment. Did he not declare in one of his ringing speeches in the stormy session of the Scottish parliament of 1703, 'It is not the prerogative of a king of Scotland I would diminish but the prerogative of English ministers over this nation'?[1] One is tempted to ask — what has changed? He also envisaged a new and juster association of the nations of Europe, the very question which heads our political agenda today. Fletcher, as well as being a great Scot, was also a great European.

Indeed, on the fundamental issues that exercised Andrew Fletcher, and in particular the good government and well-being of his native land, little seems to have changed. Forms and terminology have changed, but little of substance.

My given theme is 'patriotism'. Fletcher in his lifetime, and ever since, has always been regarded as the quintessential Scottish patriot. His character has never been better summed up than by the eighteenth-century historian, Thomas Somerville, minister of Jedburgh, who, though of unionist sympathies, wrote that Fletcher's character and parts 'exalt him to a high rank in the list of names which do honour to human nature'. But Somerville's toryism compelled him to add, 'though his ideas were chimerical'.[2] As to his ideas being chimerical, perhaps; but not for nothing has the Home Rule movement in Scotland from its effective beginnings in the 1880s found in Fletcher one of its main sources of inspiration. Thus when we speak of Andrew Fletcher today we automatically think of patriotism. It seems the only right context for him. Andrew Fletcher is, or was, the great national patriot of Scotland; just as William Wallace was the great national hero.

But there is a difficulty here. Notice my uncertainty of tense 'is or was'. That arises from the fact that things are not what they used to be, either in Scotland or in the world at large. To the generality, heroes and patriots are clean out of fashion and regarded as rather infantile figments of the imagination. The supposition seems to be that mature and sophisticated people (such as we undoubtedly are, ladies and gentlemen) need less sentimental totems. Our gradgrind generation, after over a decade of handbagging, has no time for sentiment or mush like that — unless, of course, islands on the outer rim of our globe or the essential oil of the Persian Gulf are under threat. Then what a sudden change there is! But, of course, all the resulting claptrap has little, if anything, to do with true patriotism.

Apart from those carefully orchestrated fits of hysteria,

patriotism as a concept is no longer in fashion. Indeed, except when foreign policy blunders necessitate a spate of gung-ho rubbish, politicians will assure us blandly that patriotism is just a lot of outmoded nonsense. Confronted by any patriotic notion that seems to threaten their votes, our politicos can be relied upon to quote Samuel Johnson, he whom Boswell deified, to the effect that 'patriotism is the last refuge of a scoundrel'. The trouble with our parliament people is that, addicted though they are to clichés, they rarely understand them. This one means the opposite of what it says. Indeed, Johnson, a sturdy English patriot of the John Bull type, was hitting out at mealy-mouthed politicians who used the cloak of patriotism to conceal their own evil purposes.[3]

How, then, is patriotism to be defined? The proper definition is 'disinterested love of one's country'; not uncritical love, but disinterested love. It has nothing to do with chauvinism or jingoism.

Andrew Fletcher was a true patriot. He was never a patriot out of self-interest. He was not a political looter or pillager. He was no corrupt Scotchman on the make. That is the central and astounding fact about him. Almost alone of the leading politicians of the corrupt age in which he lived Andrew Fletcher emerges spotless. I repeat, this is an astounding fact. Not a hint of corruption, not a breath of scandal, tarnishes his political reputation or sullies his fame. He aimed steadily and consistently at what he judged to be best for his country, and he allowed nothing to divert him from that course. Anyone who has studied the period that produced the Treaty and Acts of Union of 1707 must find this truly remarkable. It is the secret of his abiding appeal.

But all this is hard to accept today. We live in an age that has been traumatised into cynicism. We suspect politicians who strike moral postures. We know only too well that politicians today, like civil servants, are classical economists with the truth. Fletcher was a truthful man. He never paltered with the truth, however hard or unpleasant he, and others too, might find it. If a thing was true it had to be told. He never sought refuge in bland, meaningless banalities. He was that rare curiosity — a person of great intellect with moral stature to match, and the courage, come what might, to speak his mind.

At a time when other Scottish politicians saw their country as a bargaining counter for their own future prospects, Fletcher stood virtually alone in defending its independence. He did this not for any ulterior purpose, but in the hope of reforming its government and improving the prospects of an entire nation. One after another he saw his former allies succumb to government bribery and patronage. That was no course for him. The gulf between Andrew Fletcher and such self-seeking magnates as the Union Duke of Queensberry (who was a by-word for corruption in an age of corruption) and the Duke of Hamilton (who was notorious for his selfish twisting) was vast and unbridgeable. This I must stress. Rigorous examination of the sources and the most searching assessment of the evidence (and that has been done repeatedly of late) has unassailably demonstrated Fletcher's political integrity. The case for Fletcher's integrity is established beyond all possibility of dispute.

This means that for those of the unionist persuasion Andrew Fletcher is a bitter pill to swallow. They have to acknowledge his honesty, and by implication accept the dishonesty of others whom they would fain revere. But they console themselves with the thought that, when all is said and done, the man was a failure. They delude themselves. The writings and the ideas of Andrew Fletcher live. They come readily to hand in David Daiches's excellent book on Fletcher. But who now goes for political inspiration to the second Duke of Queensberry? Not even the most dedicated unionist today can do that.

Andrew Fletcher, then, was a great and disinterested patriot who put the needs of his country first. He did not do this out of blind, unreflecting obstinacy. Nor was it ever the case with him of 'my country, right or wrong'. Fletcher's patriotism was the product of deep reflection. He was an accomplished scholar and a profound student of political science, as well as being a man of great probity and moral courage.

That he also possessed physical courage even the most cursory survey of his life will reveal. But he was no plaster saint. He had serious temperamental defects. Pride, even arrogance, are plain to see in his character. Often he was the prisoner of his own idealism. He was also hot-tempered and prone to over-react to events. Those very defects saved his life during Monmouth's Rebellion in 1685. While taking part in that forlorn venture he shot to death a comrade who, he felt, had insulted him. Because of this he had to quit Monmouth's army and flee abroad, a move that probably saved his life for, had he survived Monmouth's defeat at Sedgemoor, he would most likely have fallen victim to the Bloody Assize presided over by Judge Jeffreys.

Fletcher, then, was no closet patriot. His deeds of valour were not confined to his writing or speechifying. He knew what he believed in, and he was prepared not only to argue for it but to hazard his life for it if need be. We can, I think, only conclude that he deserves his reputation as the great Scottish patriot.

But true patriotism, at any time, is not the monopoly of any individual or party. People learn from each other and Andrew Fletcher was fortunate to have Gilbert Burnet as a tutor. Burnet (1643-1715) was another prominent Scot of that day and age whose influence radiated far beyond the parish of Saltoun where he was minister from 1665 to 1669. He inbued Sir Robert Fletcher's heir with a love of learning and of truth.

Bishop Burnet, as he later became, is often dismissed today as a bumptious busybody and the vain prattling historian of his times. Now, undoubtedly, Gibbie had 'a guid conceit o' himsel'; but he was also a man of rare abilities and of superior moral qualities.

Though a sincere episcopalian, Burnet criticised the harsh political episcopacy imposed upon Scotland after the Restoration in 1660. He supported the efforts made by Bishop Robert Leighton of Dunblane to secure an accommodation between episcopalians and presbyterians. He became friendly with James, Duke of York, the heir to the throne who, perhaps for his own ulterior motives as a crypto-catholic, also desired toleration. The friendship soon

foundered after James became an open catholic, for Burnet dreaded
and feared papistry. All the same, at a time when it was dangerous
to do so, he defended catholics who were threatened in the hysteria
raised by the lying tales of Titus Oates about the so-called Popish
Plot. Burnet also tried to mediate in the Exclusion Bill crisis when
efforts were made to prevent the succession of the catholic Duke
of York. Eager to secure such a redoubtable champion, Charles II,
who loyally maintained his brother's right to succeed, offered
Burnet the bishopric of Chichester if he would fully support the
Court. It was a glittering prize to dangle before such a young and
highly ambitious man. Nonetheless, the offer was spurned, and a
little later Burnet wrote to Charles II condemning the king's vicious
life. Burnet spelled it out, as few men in that age of shameless time-
serving would have dared to do: 'You have,' he told the king, 'not
served God, but, have given yourself up to so many sinful pleasures'.[4]
Rarely can a divine-right monarch have been so addressed by a
humble divine. In fairness, however, it should be said, that, if it
was admirable for Burnet to write so frankly, it was also admirable
for Charles II to feel no more than a momentary annoyance with
this outspoken Scottish parson.

Nevertheless, beneath the brash and vain exterior of the
Buzzard, as Dryden memorably satirised him in *The Hind and the
Panther*, Burnet's life shows a consistent blend of courage and
integrity. Thus, in November 1684 when the succession of the
catholic Duke of York was imminent, Burnet preached against it
on the text 'Save me from the lion's mouth'. That took courage.
And shortly after James's accession to the throne in February 1685
Burnet was forced to join those who were obliged to tarry abroad.
He ultimately took refuge in Holland, just as his old pupil Andrew
Fletcher had to do. Burnet, indeed, became a chaplain to William
of Orange and landed with 'the Great Deliverer' at Torbay on 5
November 1688, as did Fletcher. Burnet's advice helped to secure
the Revolution Settlement in England, though he was rendered
uneasy by the more radical settlement accomplished in his native
Scotland. He became Bishop of Salisbury, a stalwart for the

Protestant Succession and a champion of the House of Hanover. In all this he stood up for the rights of Scotland. In March 1705 he argued in the House of Lords for union but deplored the ill-government Scotland had been under since 1603, and sought to take the sting out of the Alien Act.[5] But here Burnet's position differed from that of Fletcher, and he went on to support the Treaty of Union of 1707, which, he felt, secured the religion, liberties and prosperity of Scotland. In this matter he was, if you like, Mr Worldly Wiseman to Fletcher's mystic visionary.

But that, perhaps, is a rather facile judgement. For, take him all in all, Gilbert Burnet was a sincere patriot whose love for his native land was not extinguished by his wider British patriotism.[6] He simply differed from his old pupil, Andrew Fletcher, on how best to secure his country's interests. Burnet's support for the Union sprang from conviction and was not secured by bribery, a fact that was appreciated by many of his countrymen. True, to the Jacobites Burnet was a complete snake-in-the-grass, but they detested anyone who did not idolise the house of Stewart. Of the anti-Stewart faction only Fletcher won and held their regard. Others were more objective than the Jacobites. In 1705, for example, James Anderson, the patriotic Scots antiquary, and a presbyterian to boot, described Gilbert Burnet as follows, 'Dr Burnet, now Bishop of Sarum, one of the Great Ornaments of the Reform'd Church, and of our Countrey'.[7] It was a just verdict on a much maligned scholar and man of affairs.

What I am suggesting here is that people can differ about the national good and what best serves its interests. Consequently, it is unrealistic to adhere rigidly to one criterion of patriotism to the exclusion of all others. Consider an even more provocative case, that of Sir George Mackenzie of Rosehaugh (1636?-1691). We are apt to believe that Andrew Fletcher of Saltoun and Sir George Mackenzie of Rosehaugh must have shared nothing but a mutual detestation, the one an intrepid patriot and sea-green incorruptible, and the other the brutal time-serving lackey of a cruel despotism. In fact, we know nothing of their personal relationship, if indeed they had one. Certainly Mackenzie as Lord Advocate prosecuted

Fletcher for treason in 1685-6, but the conviction was secured in the absence of the accused.[8] From a study of their careers, however, it emerges that they had some powerful bonds in common. Each had a fearless patriotism, and each showed similar personal traits. They both had strong, thrusting, aggressive personalities, and both combined keen intelligence and great learning with high physical courage. Neither was in the least burdened with modesty. They were men of powerful passions and adamantine convictions. And central to all their endeavours was what they took to be the good of their country.

Saltoun and Rosehaugh do seem an unlikely constellation. But the more you get beneath the surface of their times, the more clear it becomes that they represented the last age of pure and unalloyed Scottish patriotism, just as Burnet pioneers the North British brand. That is an easy thesis to maintain as far as Fletcher is concerned. His whole life sustains that conclusion. But can it possibly be true of 'the Bluidy Advocate'? Has not the genius of Scott in 'Wandering Willie's Tale' depicted Mackenzie forever as the demigod of the unholy crew of persecutors of the saints of the Covenant?[9] There is no time here to go into details, but being the scourge of the Covenanters was only part of Mackenzie's varied career. Other parts can be cited to prove that Mackenzie was a patriot.

Consider the trifling matter of the 45 kings. In the mid 1680s Mackenzie furiously attacked the works of Bishop William Lloyd and Dr Edward Stillingfleet, Englishmen who had dared to reject the early history of Scotland, as given by Hector Boece, and who ruthlessly jettisoned the mysterious 45 ancient kings of Scots who stretched from Fergus I, said to have flourished about 330 BC, to Fergus mor mac Erc, circa 500 AD. According to Mackenzie, stout royalist and staunch episcopalian that he was, Bishop Lloyd verged on treason in thus truncating the royal line. Indeed, claimed Mackenzie, if the Bishop of St Asaph dared to repeat such assertions in Scotland it would be his duty as Lord Advocate of His Majesty's ancient kingdom to prosecute the bishop for leasing-making, then a capital charge as the case of the unfortunate Earl of Argyll had just proved in 1681.

The truth is that Mackenzie of Rosehaugh was a man of principles, but curiously ill-assorted and sometimes apparently contradictory principles. He was a royalist and unshakable in his legitimist beliefs. Here he differed totally from Fletcher. But at the same time Mackenzie was a firm believer in the law and in legal government. He was also a champion of the rights of parliament. In his *Memoirs on the Affairs of Scotland* he is rather critical of the wholesale jettisoning in 1661 of the constitutional reforms that had been carried out by the Covenanters.[10] He certainly detested the Covenanters, mainly as flouters of the law, but held little brief for the corrupt practices of the Restoration regime. In his book, *The Religious Stoic*, he wrote: 'I take the laws of my country to be my creed.' Nor did he ever lose his belief in the rights of the parliament of Scotland. In 1670 he was one of the few who defied the court and was critical of the incorporating union then proposed.[11] In his *Life* of Mackenzie, Andrew Lang declared of this episode, that Mackenzie 'would have been, from patriotic motives, on the side of Lockhart of Carnwath and Fletcher of Saltoun, against the Union, had he lived to take part in the debates of 1706'. [12] The speculation seems reasonable.

Mackenzie of Rosehaugh opposed incorporating union with England, partly on nationalist grounds and partly because it would have meant the end of the Scottish parliament. This, in turn, would have posed threats to the continuance of Scots Law. Mackenzie contributed greatly to the development of Scots Law and dreaded lest it should be supplanted by what he took to be the inferior English legal system. [13] As an expounder and shaper of the Law of Scotland Sir George Mackenzie of Rosehaugh ranks second only to his great contemporary and rival, Sir James Dalrymple of Stair himself.

In keeping with his legitimist principles, Mackenzie opposed the Revolution of 1689. The fall of the bishops in Scotland confirmed his opposition to the Revolution. There is some evidence to suggest that if episcopacy in Scotland had survived Mackenzie might have accepted William and Mary. [14] But it was not to be. The bishops paltered with William and destroyed their church. Such a Scotland was no place for Mackenzie, who spent much of the last two years of his life in Oxford. There in that home of lost causes and port and prejudice he played the role of the mature student, enjoying the run of the Bodleian and the college libraries. The 'noble wit of Scotland,' as Dryden called him, relished, too, the sparkling conversation for which Oxford was, and still is, renowned. During his lost days in England he held friendly converse with his old adversary, Bishop Lloyd, who had defied James II and who had prospered under the new order. The friendship of Lloyd and Mackenzie is a salutary reminder that bitter literary controversies do not inevitably mean murderous personal relations.

I submit that the careers of these three gifted but very different Scotsmen (Fletcher, Burnet and Mackenzie) were all shaped by patriotic zeal. True patriotism, I repeat, is not the monopoly of any one party or faction, as the diverse careers of the royalist Mackenzie and the radical Fletcher reveal. And the career of Gilbert Burnet cannot convincingly be seen as a monument to self-interest.

I would suggest that the common bond was a recognition of their nationality, and a deep and pure love of their country. Nationhood is not just an abstract philosophical concept. It rests on shared sentiment, a belief in the past and a hope for the future. It is a given fact, and, though it is difficult to define, it is deep rooted in reality. The history of Scotland has provided innumerable examples of the durability of this sense of Scottish identity. I will not weary you with a list of familiar examples, but I would like to draw your attention to a remarkable instance that deserves to be better known.

It is to be found in Alexander Kinglake's *Eothen*, impressions of travels in the Near East in 1835-6. After much toil Kinglake reached Cairo and sought lodgings from one Osman Effendi, who owned several houses. He did not seek in vain, Osman falling over himself to be obliging. Kinglake explains why. Says he, 'Osman's history is a curious one. He was a Scotchman born, and when very young, being then a drummer-boy he landed in Egypt with Fraser's force'.

This was a botched expedition to seize Alexandria in 1807, and, continues Kinglake, the unfortunate drummer-boy was taken prisoner. He was presented with the usual choice — death or the Koran — and, as Kinglake laconically put it, 'he did not choose death'. He was forced to campaign against the Wahabees, those puritanical covenanters of Islam; he prospered and acquired properties, including two wives. He invited Kinglake to see his hareem but kept his wives out of the way, mainly, Kinglake surmised, somewhat ungallantly, because they were not too well favoured. Then comes the really remarkable part of this unusual tale. Let me give you it in Kinglake' s own words.

> But the strangest feature in Osman's character was his inextinguishable nationality. In vain they had brought him over the seas in early boyhood— in vain had he suffered captivity, conversion, circumcision — in vain they had passed him through fire in their Arabian campaigns — they could not cut away or burn out poor Osman's love of all that was Scotch; in vain men called him Effendi — in vain he swept along in Eastern robes — in vain the rival wives adorned his hareem; the joy of his heart still plainly lay in this, that he had three shelves of books, and that the books were thoroughbred Scotch — the Edinburgh this — the Edinburgh that — and, above all, I recollect that he prided himself upon 'the Edinburgh Cabinet Library'. [15]

From General David Stewart of Garth we learn that Osman had been a drummer-boy in the 78th Ross-shire Highlanders, that his name was Macleod and that he had enlisted at Perth. He had learnt something of the surgeon's craft by assisting the regimental surgeon and had become a successful, though unqualified, physician in Cairo. From information received Stewart says that Macleod, 'being very handsome, made a respectable appearance in his Turkish robes and turban'.[16]

How, I wonder, would Fletcher have reacted to Osman Effendi? His feelings, I think, would have been mixed, for although Fletcher of Saltoun was not a religious fanatic he cared greatly for the concept of Christendom. He was a firm European and had an almost

Crusader-like faith in Christendom and the need to defend it from aggressive Islam. During his exile he soldiered in Hungary against the Turks who were then threatening Vienna. So he would probably have felt that Osman had made the wrong choice and should have died honourably rather than accept the Koran. But, at the same time, Fletcher would have understood and applauded Osman's undying Scottishness.

Both Mackenzie of Rosehaugh and Fletcher of Saltoun were enthralled by the same powerful force as poor Osman Effendi. To them nationhood was a cardinal fact of life, and as such could not be denied. They believed that the nationhood of Scotland was a historic fact of longstanding, and that the only sane thing to do about that historic fact was to accept it and to build on it. To do any other was to break faith and store up trouble for the future.

Let me end by recalling the last words of Andrew Fletcher. They are well attested by two contemporary sources. A letter from Sir Hugh Paterson to the exiled Earl of Mar, the 'Bobbing John' of the '15, written at Leyden on 9 October 1716, says that, 'The last words he spoke were "My Poor Country" ', and that he had left £200 to help the Jacobite prisoners of the late rebellion.[17] Saltoun's last words were also reported more immediately and fully by his nephew, also named Andrew Fletcher, who, such is the irony of fate, later became an 18th-century grafting politician of considerable note. Young Andrew, the Lord Milton that was to be, was at his uncle's death-bed in London, and in a letter home he described his uncle's last hours. Wrote young Andrew: 'I thought he said I forgive everybody, and wish everybody may forgive me; about a quarter of an hour thereafter he said distinctly, Lord have mercy on my poor Countrey that is so barbarously oppressed'.[18]

It seems to me that those last words of the great Scottish patriot have a melancholy resonance to this day.

References

1   David Daiches, ed., *Andrew Fletcher of Saltoun. Selected Political Writings and Speeches* (Edinburgh. 1979), p.80.
2   Thomas Somerville, *The History of Great Britain during the Reign of Queen Anne* (London, 1798), p.204.
3   James Boswell, *The Life of Samuel Johnson* (Everyman edition, 1910), volume I, pp 547-8.
4   T.E.S Clarke and H.C. Foxcroft, *A life of Gilbert Burnet, Bishop of Salisbury* (Cambridge, 1907), p.160.
5   Ibid., pp 412-3.
6   Ibid., pp 480-1.
7   James Anderson, *Historical Essay shewing that the Crown and Kingdom of Scotland is Imperial and Independent* (Edinburgh, 1705), p.42.
8   T.B Howell, *State Trials*, volume XI, cols 1023-1057.
9   Sir Walter Scott, *Redgauntlet*, Letter XI.
10 Sir George Mackenzie of Rosehaugh, *Memoirs of the Affairs of Scotland from the Restoration of King Charles II, AD 1660*, (Edinburgh, 1821), p.21.
11 Ibidem, pp 185-7, 211-12
12 Andrew Lang, *Sir George Mackenzie, King's Advocate, of Rosehaugh. His Life and Times 1636(?)-1691* (London, 1909), p.93.
13 See David M. Walker, *The Scottish Jurists* (Edinburgh, 1985), chapter 9, pp. 158-172.
14 See *The Diary of John Evelyn*, ed. E.S. de Beer (Oxford, 1955), volume IV, pp 614-5.
15 Alexander William Kinglake, *Eothen* (Everyman, 1928), chapter 18, pp. 156-7.
16 Colonel David Stewart, *Sketches of the Character, Manners and Present State of the Highlanders of Scotland* (Edinburgh, 1977 reprint), II, p.281.
17 W. C. Mackenzie, *Andrew Fletcher of Saltoun. His Life and Times* (London, 1935), p.310.
18 *Miscellany of the Scottish History Society, volume X* (Edinburgh, 1965). 'Letters of Andrew Fletcher of Saltoun and his family 1715-16', edited by Irene J. Murray, p.171.

1992

The Constitutional Options

Iain Noble

Sir Iain Noble is a merchant banker and business man, and, in 1992 was executive Chairman (and founder) of Noble and Company Limited, merchant bankers, Edinburgh. He is a campaigner for Scottish culture in general and the Gaelic language in particular. He was President of The Saltire Society from 1993 to 96.

The Constitutional Options

Iain Noble

"I stand for nationality and the simple human things which are its roots' said Sir Harry Lauder — like Andrew Fletcher an East Lothian man.

The consciousness of nationality in Scotland has continued for three centuries since Andrew Fletcher's day, and was not extinguished by the Act of Union. When they register at an hotel most Scotsmen still state their nationality as 'Scottish', whereas most English ones nowadays describe themselves as 'British'. The same spirit which inspired Andrew Fletcher's campaign in the Scots parliament between 1703 and 1707 is alive in our day.

It is important to emphasise at this point that my theme today is not intended to have any party political bias. I have no allegiances on party lines nor do I have a great desire to participate in party politics. Listening to politicians in action it is sometimes difficult to restrain a feeling of despair. So many of them seem to consider it more important to insult their political foes than to generate their own constructive ideas.

But that is an aside. This address will focus on the constitutional issue in Scotland as a matter of public concern, as seen from a purely personal viewpoint. It has been too much the subject of political jockeying from a party political point or view, and has not received nearly enough general objective analysis.

Paul Scott's splendid and well researched book *Andrew Fletcher and the Treaty of Union* which has just been published vividly describes a Scotland which is past, Scotland in a confused state, but a country proud of its history, its distinctive culture, famous already for its innovative skills, its sophisticated financial institutions, an advanced legal system and the highest standard of education in Europe, as well as a sense of democracy and egalitarian spirit unusual for its time. Sir John Fortescue commented as early as the 15th century that 'by ancient customs a King of Scots may not rule his people by other laws than they assent to'. These features do not marry well with the modern popular perception of Scotland as a country which has always been backward and impoverished!

The world may change, but nationality survives the world over. Look at Norway which ceased to exist in the 15th century, yet reappeared honourably in response to democratic wishes in 1900 more than four centuries later. Hungary lost is independence for hundreds of years until it re-emerged in 1919, its sense of nationality seemingly undiminished.

Today, alongside the continuing instinct to form huge new conglomerations both of companies and of nations, we also freely recognise the philosophy that 'small is beautiful'. In the business world we encourage entrepreneurs and new business start-ups as important for commercial vigour, we accept the benefits of MBOs (or management buyouts) as a means of re-stimulating subsidiaries which have lost their drive.

In the political world the modern state professes the spirit of democracy as a creed, and most people applaud the courage of Latvia, Lithuania and Estonia. What are these but political MBOs? Perhaps we respect the Bosnians and Croatians too though we fear greatly for communities where racial hatred goes far beyond the boundaries of Christian tolerance.

Andrew Fletcher of Saltoun, known as 'The Patriot', the scholar, would have agreed, that the instinct to reform national boundaries where there is a strong sense of community need is not unworthy or in any way dishonourable. We all understand that instinct and it applies as much in politics as in business. Whether the instinct is wise, rash, impetuous in any particular case is another question, but it is not dishonourable. It is often described as patriotism. Isn't it interesting that Governments are willing enough to revise internal local authority boundaries but are remarkably sensitive and reluctant about revising their own?

However it is not wise to suppress strong community desires. We have seen in history, ancient and modern, that attempts by monarchs, dictators and even parliamentary governments to suppress a strong community desire for change can lead in the end to rebellions, revolutions, and anarchy. The anarchy which can result from thwarted community pressure may bring in its wake confusion for decades. Those who lead 'revolutions' often forget that the cure can be worse than the disease.

The pure instincts of nationality, like religion and also membership of a football club, are capable of creating blind loyalty which is altogether oblivious to reason. I remember my tutor in logic once telling to me when asked to explain the rationale of some aspect of religion 'where God comes in obligation to explain goes out'. Nationality likewise is a strong emotional instinct which can fly far beyond logic.

Yet it also is a powerful instrument which can bring out great reserves of energy, excitement, enthusiasm and confidence, beneficial to any community when applied wisely and purposefully. 'All the great deeds of history' it is said 'are the result of strong emotions early implanted'.

A *deja vue* attitude already colours our reflections on the dominant issues of the general election last May. The politicians postured pugilistically, yet the strands of the argument stand out clear: the sense of nationality in Scotland has not evaporated, the debate continues as to whether Westminster has an obligation to recognise the apparent democratic desire of the Scots for autonomy, a consistent and recurring feature of the last hundred years.

A government which refuses to allow any autonomy in Scotland in such circumstances can hardly claim to be an 'understanding' government. Is credit to be found in resisting the tenets of democracy? Will this response be interpreted in the future 'as excessive possessiveness?'

The argument that it is difficult to create a suitable

constitutional framework within the UK, referred to as 'The West Lothian Question', is not easy to sustain. Where there is a will there is a way and after all there are already UK precedents in the Isle of Man and the Channel Islands, as well as many examples elsewhere in the world of which Spain is a very relevant illustration.

During the election campaign I thought I detected an interesting shift in the nature of the Great Debate compared with a decade or two ago. At that time the home rule campaigners seemed to be driven mainly from the heart. Recently home rulers appear to rely less on purely emotional arguments and focus more on more practical down to earth ones.

But on the other hand the reaction south of the Border has gradually moved from original scepticism to serious concern, more defensive with definitely detectable emotional overtones. The 'emotion' seems to have moved south!

Nowhere is this more clearly demonstrated than in the 'slippery slope' arguments used to resist the popular campaign in Scotland, as if to say 'we might not mind a bit of autonomy but we know that when you get a taste of it you will want more, and therefore we won't make any concessions at all'.

If belief in democracy were paramount creed it would be more appropriate to say 'yes you may have some autonomy, why not start with a little, if it works and you like it you will be better able to judge whether or not you yourselves want more, or prefer to remain together with the rest of us: in any case a step by step procedure is wisest as you do not yet have the experience of running a country or the necessary institutions with a track record, both of which are important features of a successful democratic system. Did we not put forward exactly these ideas as part of the process of handing back independence to colonies of the old British Empire?'

May I be excused for touching on specific political parties, for there is a puzzling enigma. The SNP has been trying to capture votes from the Labour Party on the grounds that the latter are the dominant party here, but why? Labour supports home rule.

The Tories, although they were the first party to put forward plans for an Assembly, have withdrawn from the field under Thatcher and left a vacuum. Yet it appears that more than half of those who vote Tory in Scotland favour some sort of home rule. I am sure there are many other conservatively minded people who would vote Tory if the Scottish Tory Party was seen to be more amenable to democratic public opinion and less under the thumb of Central Office in London.

A vacuum on the right wing of Scottish politics is therefore created by the entrenched left wing policies of the SNP on the one hand and the inflexible Unionist stance of the Tories on the other. Yet it would be most undesirable for any Scottish Parliament to emerge say after the next election with no significant grouping to represent right of centre views. The problem is accentuated because the SNP have not succeeded in winning the support of the business and professional communities and I believe this has proved to be their Achilles heel. In a world where jobs are a major issue, how can you expect the ordinary citizen to vote for a platform which the business community rejects so strongly.

Does this mean there is a need for a new right wing Scottish party? Or will the Scottish Tory organisation loosen its links with the Central Office in London, run up the democratic flag, and support home rule in order to appeal better to the ordinary conservatively minded Scottish voter? Or will the SNP be able to persuade the business community that autonomy really is their interest? Surely with the business sector in support, pressures for home rule would be very hard to resist. Who therefore will fill this vacuum?

However we must ask ourselves why the business world has been so unreceptive to home rule. It is true that businessmen do not generally like changes in legislation. They have learned to live with the status quo and do not want to relearn the rules unless there are good reasons. They have accepted pretty universally the pronouncements that Scotland would be more highly taxed and that some businesses might move out. Many are nervous of domination by left wing politics, which are traditionally considered to be unfriendly towards industry. Business people all over the world do not seem to like left wing governments.

How much more convincing the SNP campaign would have been if they could have dealt with these fears by demonstrating that autonomy in Scotland would be an exciting opportunity from a commercial point of view. How much more convincing the Scottish Tory party would have been if it had been more attuned to the obvious claims of democracy.

It has almost become received wisdom, that Scotland would be more highly taxed as it receives more than its due share of the UK governmental budget. Well, in the first place, cognoscenti agree that it is certainly not clear whether Scotland gets more than its fair share. Insufficient statistics are available and government figures refer only to what they call 'identifiable public expenditure' which excludes some major items, notably defence, and no doubt the cost of central government administration.

A second point is more intriguing. Even if it were true that Scotland gets slightly more than its per capita share of government expenditure, would taxation be higher in Scotland? I believe it need not be. For one thing expenditure which is managed nearer home should be better and less expensively administered, more appropriately allocated and generally better spent. Less money should be needed to achieve the same results.

However I would like to put forward another proposition which is that it is axiomatic that whatever colour of government is elected to a Scottish parliament, it would soon discover that a tax level higher than in England would be self defeating. There would be an immediate flow of capital out of Scotland and a migration of ambitious people and higher tax payers. The resulting capital drain and brain drain would be very damaging to the commercial fabric of the country. No, that will not work.

On the other hand if tax rates are set lower than in England the opposite will happen. Multinational and pan-UK companies which always have some discretion in this respect, will so arrange their affairs that their profits will as far as possible be generated in their

Scottish operations rather than in any higher tax regime.

Attraction of industry to Scotland would be easier. An inflow of able people should result which I would describe as a 'brain tap'. Those higher tax payers who can do so will tend to move to Scotland bringing with them taxable revenues.

In short the Scottish exchequer will raise more revenue by ensuring that tax rates are lower in Scotland, and will raise less revenue if tax rates in Scotland are higher. So the only practical stance would be lower tax rates. The question is whether the right stance would be for taxes in Scotland to be say 10% lower than in England, or whether a Channel Islands or Swiss formula with a very low tax regime would produce an even greater harvest of state revenue in the end. I imagine the commercial community would not object to becoming part of a lower tax regime

Of course I have not touched on the question of oil reserves, though in the event of leaving the UK altogether this should bring a useful short term financial boost to underwrite the launching period, but that is not a subject to dwell on here.

The business world is used to the idea of MBOs as a way of breathing new life into jaded subsidiary businesses. They have a number of advantages. For example they tend to eliminate a level of parent company overheads and administrative costs which can make the subsidiary viable in a manner not previously possible. They offer stronger motivation and incentives for management, whose renewed enthusiasm can be harnessed: enthusiasm is the work horse of success when it is applied in the right way. Home rule in Scotland could be regarded as a kind of political MBO, generating enthusiasm and achieving administrative economies. Of course London is an expensive city in which to locate the UK's political 'Head Office', and of course Edinburgh would gain by becoming a genuine capital.

Yes on balance I think a good case can be made to the Scottish business sector to show that they could benefit from having a sensible parliament, a political MBO, and I believe they would more easily understand this if the fear of permanent domination by a too left wing government could be diminished.

Where do we go from here? Let's leave out the current emotive terminology and not use words like 'devolution' or 'separation'. There appear to be four main options for Scotland, namely the status quo, home rule within a UK framework, home rule within an EC framework ('autonomy within Europe') or de-merging from both UK and the rest of Europe. Let us look at each of these briefly.

Option 1, the status quo, has some arguments in its favour. On the whole people prefer stability. The devil you know is usually preferable to the devil you don't. We have many business ties with England and our laws have been largely synchronised. We have relations and friends there. Many English live among us. History has bound us together for 285 years. However the public in Scotland do not want it, about three quarters of us want the right to do things differently, and to preserve our identity. We do not want to be homogenised into a British/English porridge. For anyone who believes in democracy the status quo is hardly an honourable option unless public opinion changes sharply.

Option 2: Home Rule in the UK. This has been dogged by the 'West Lothian Question' though as already mentioned the Channel Islands and the Isle of Man are precedents which could he duplicated with variations. That would mean foreign policy dealt with in London but virtually everything else in Scotland. Spain is also an example because it is divided federally into different states, with varying degrees of autonomy. The Faroe Islands is part of Denmark and sends MPs to Denmark, yet it is the only part of Denmark which has its own parliament with wide discretion over local affairs. Politicians who say that the constitutional problems are insuperable are talking through their hats.

Home Rule within the UK has another advantage that we would learn to walk gradually, as already described. In theory, Scotland could later choose whether to go for increased autonomy, or retain the relationship with England. This option has the great advantage of being cautious and prudent (traditional Scottish virtues) and responding to a clear democratic wish. It has many attractions.

The third option is Home Rule within Europe. This too has attractions since it implies removing an expensive layer of government in London, a direct input of views into Europe and an opportunity to press vigorously in Brussels on issues which are important in Scotland such as fishing, agriculture, forestry and other natural resources where Scotland is self sufficient but England is a major importer.

Note that if Scotland were an autonomous unit of the EEC, the number of UK MPs in the European Parliament would increase. At present Scotland has fewer Euro MPs than Denmark which has a similar population (eight versus sixteen). Even Luxembourg which has a population of only 300,000 people has six, almost as many as we do. Thus the UK voice in Europe would be strengthened, and in view of our close ties through history, business, kith and kin, it is hard to believe that we will not have similar views on most matters to those of our southern neighbours. If Westminster is polite to the Scots it could have a louder shout in Brussels.

There is also another tempting, intriguing but probably fanciful angle. Could it be that independence in Scotland would diminish tension in the land of our ancient cousins in Hibernia? Would Ireland feel more comfortable when not 'surrounded' by the UK on all sides, but part of say a loose federation within the British Isles, a sort of Benelux? A wonderful prospect if it could be realised but alas it can at best be a far away hope.

Where then are the disadvantages of Home Rule in Europe one might ask? It would certainly be a bigger step into the unknown than Home Rule in the UK. The benefit of a gradual learning process would disappear. If we have the confidence there is no reason why we should not face this more ambitious challenge, but if we are mice we will naturally prefer to stay behind the skirting board.

But what about Europe and what sort of an organisation would we be joining? Would we be jumping out of the frying pan into the fire? We do not yet know whether Mastricht will proceed. Even if it does, we do not know whether Brussels will eventually become as centralised as London. More importantly we really do not know how Europe will turn out. It could be an explosive mixture, a Pandora's box from which all the evil winds emerge when the lid is opened. Is it possible for harmony to prevail among so many countries with different languages, history and culture? Races do not mingle easily and permanently and problems could brew at any time.

Even Belgium is in tension between Flemish and Walloons, and Yugoslavia is a timely reminder that an artificial political unit is a tinder box. Is Europe governable without a common language, and which countries will permit their languages to disappear in favour of uniformity? I doubt this will be an easy process, and assimilation in Europe could bring savage retribution to its creators within a generation or two.

Option 4: What about total demerging from both England and Europe? Most people shudder at this proposal but it does have some attractions. We could be to Europe what Hong Kong is to China, what the Channel Islands are to London, Monaco to France, Switzerland to the rest of Europe, Singapore to the rest of Asia. Being a small community on the edge of a very big one, there are ways in which we could use proximity to live off morsels from the dripping roast. Moreover Scotland has few enemies in the world, and a popular reputation internationally which could be an advantage.

However there is no doubt that total separation from the UK and Europe would be a high risk strategy. Many Scottish companies do a majority of their business outside Scotland, and customs barriers might be erected against them. Some American companies have located in Scotland to serve the European market, and they might well move to a new location within the EC boundary. The strategy might work in the end, but would be painful in the beginning. Unless we had a free trade arrangement with the EC It is hard to see it as a serious option.

There is actually a fifth option, though an eccentric one: to detach ourselves from England and join some other country such as France. A pretty unrealistic one it has to be admitted, but it did happen in our history once before when Scotland and France became a joint Kingdom, and it is true that England has been economically one of the less successful countries of Europe this century. Would our prosperity be greater as part of France, or as a Saxon off shore island of the German Republic? Of course you will tell me that this is entirely a non-starter in the present climate, and although I enjoy what is called lateral thinking, who could possibly disagree with you?

What conclusions should we draw from this? This review seems to suggest that if in Scotland we have sufficient confidence in ourselves, we should be looking seriously at either home rule within the UK or home rule within Europe. However more investigation is needed, of a sensible and preferably not a political kind.

However please note that it is official policy to break up business monopolies and the Monopolies Commission exists for this purpose. It is said that monopolies dull the spirit of innovation, and exploit absence of competition. Home rule could bring the benefits of dismantling a political monopoly, providing diversity of ideas, competition, experimentation. Home rule should be right in the spirit of the Government's own anti-monopolistic policies!

Nevertheless creating of a parliament is not by itself an automatic success recipe. 'For forms of government let fools contest, What e'er is best administered is best' in the words of Pope. Good leadership is the secret of success. But where will that leadership come from?

Andrew Fletcher was a scholar. His library contained 10,000 volumes according to Paul Scott's book. He was universally recognized in his day for integrity and intellect. An anonymous poet said of him in 1705:

A genius past the reach of English Gold.
Great and refin'd cast in no common mould.
Were all thy Peers, oh Scotland, such as he,
It were impossible to Conquer Thee.

Those lines are as apposite today, for Scotland needs the support of its establishment, its management echelon as well as its community leaders, to make a success of autonomy. Scotland needs people of ability, statesmen of the heart as well as the head, politicians and businessmen with entrepreneurial spirit. Where is that independent entrepreneurial MBO spirit, and why has it been so slow to emerge? Who will convince our business leaders and opinion formers that there is a practical positive businesslike opportunity here, by filling that vacuum I described. That is the challenge of the next five years.

Therefore, here at the grave of Andrew Fletcher let us resolve not to cease the debate. Let us lead the debate from within Scotland for if we ourselves do not know what we want, how can we expect Westminster to decide for us. The last time that happened was on the death of Alexander III, when Edward I was invited to act as umpire and used the opportunity for his benefit.

If this long standing issue can at last be resolved, I believe it will lead to the greater peace, enrichment and contentedness of Europe, and strengthen not diminish the friendships between the communities on this island. It is right that the reasonable wishes, responsibly expressed over a long period, of an ancient people with a strong sense of nationality should be honoured and not frustrated.

May I end by saying that these are but the random reflections of one individual, a Scotsman proud of his nationality. I hope Andrew Fletcher, above, approves my theme. He, above ordinary mortals followed that biblical maxim, which is also on my great grandfather's grave 'Whatever thy hand findeth to do, do it with thy might'.

I am honoured to have had the privilege of recalling his memory today at this Saltire Society occasion and now have great pleasure in proposing a libation on the grave of the unforgettable Andrew Fletcher of Saltoun, 'the Patriot'.

1993

Scots Wha Haenae

Sheila Douglas

Dr Sheila Douglas is a teacher, singer and authority on Scottish folk-song. She has played a significant part in restoring the story telling tradition in Scotland and has produced a folktale collection *The King of the Black Art* and a children's novel, *The Magic Chanter*. She lectures on the Scottish Music course at the RSAMD and is a partner in the Merlin Press, which publishes Scots teaching material. Her other books include *The Sang's The Thing* (1992) and *Come Gie's a Sang* (1997) and she is also one of the editors of the Grieg-Duncan collection.

Scots Whae Haenae

Sheila Douglas

It was Andrew Fletcher of Saltoun who said 'I knew a man so wise who said that if he was permitted to make a nation's ballads, he would not care who made its laws.' To many people nowadays those words would sound at best meaningless, at worst crazy. A great deal of song nowadays has been either sanitised, commercialised or trivialised and seems to have little connection with what politicians like to call 'the real world.' What is 'real' of course, depends on your point of view. The real world, according to them, of course, is the market place and the only music that matters is the clatter of cash registers. The drums of war sound loud enough it's true, trying to drown out the cries of wounded children, the screams of raped women and the moans of dying men. These are the battle disharmonies, the awful discord of modern times. But these are sounds: what has happened to words and tunes? Are there words adequate to express the feelings people have about what is happening to them and their world? Are there tunes sad enough or powerful enough to endue words with fire or with efficacy? The answer is that there always have been and there always will be. Look, as Andrew Fletcher could not do, at your television screen and you will see and hear people all over the world, wherever there is conflict, injustice or a struggle for freedom — you will see and hear them singing. We have heard them in the Baltic States, in Russia, in South Africa, in Northern Ireland and in Palestine — people singing for their freedom. And that is very reassuring to those who despair of humanity, because singing is the voice of humanity.

Scotland has always been credited with being a singing nation, honoured and admired for its ballads, welcomed for its lyric or its comic songs. Both in oral tradition and in literary tradition, song has always held a high place. In collections, some of them international, Scots narrative and expressive songs have been declared the best. At this very time, the greatest song collection ever to come out of the British Isles, the Greig-Duncan collection, made in Buchan in the early 1900s, by a schoolmaster and a minister, is being published in eight mighty volumes. But wait a minute, you say, isn't that the last few remaining relics of a dying song culture made in a remote area, cut off from modern trends? Not a bit of it. You have only to look inside one volume to find the hallmark of a vigorous living tradition in the multiplicity of versions of most of the songs. The railway and turnpike roads, popular newspapers and the development of labour-intensive farming gave the area better communications and a livelier social life than ever before. The working population was well-schooled by dominies like Gavin Greig, who were also scholars, writers and educationists, and ministers like James Duncan, who were also in touch with their cultural roots, for he collected songs from his own family.

Song tradition was one aspect of Scottish culture that was not adversely affected by the Union, but actually blossomed in the 18th century and was also assiduously collected from then on, by a whole succession of literary men who were also often singers and songwriters themselves, like Ramsay, Burns, Scott, Kirkpatrick Sharpe, Maidment, Motherwell and others. As a collector myself, I can vouch for the fact that since the Greig-Duncan hairst was gathered, song tradition has not withered and died, but lives on in many parts of Scotland, on the lips of living singers, who still retain a love for their native songs, even in the teeth of pressure from the classical or pop world. There is evidence of this in my book *The Sang's the Thing*, a celebration of twenty-eight Lowland singers, their lives and their songs. Some find it quite possible to like more than one kind of music, a self-evident truth to which many people close their eyes, or should I say ears. In our tradition of course folk song has never been an inferior genre or one associated with ignorance or illiteracy. Our two best known poets and writers. Burns and Scott, were up to their eyeballs in folk tradition and many tradition bearers, past and present have been educated people. Our tradition has in other words been a shared one and a democratic one.

One of the strongest strains of Scottish song is that of satire, particularly political satire, and that goes back a long long way.

> Some say that kissin's a sin but I think it's nane ava,
> For kissin has woned in this warld since ever there wis twa.
> If it wisna lawfu, lawyers widnae allow it.
> If it wisna holy, ministers widna dae it,
> If it wisna modest, maidens widna tak it.
> If it wisna plenty, puir fowk widna get it.

At first hearing that may not strike you as a political song, just a comic ditty, with a hint of bawdry. But like the scorpion, its sting is in the tail. 'If it wisna plenty, puir fowk widna get it.' Poverty has been both the curse and the blessing of Scotland a curse for holding its people in all kinds of misery for centuries, and a blessing in that it has saved the Scottish character from the corruptions brought by affluence. But it has been and continues to be a fact of life in a country that does not lack resources. We have the land, we have the sea, we have crops and minerals, we have a skilled and educated people; yet we are poor. Scotland must be the only country in the world that has struck oil and not prospered as a result. The reason is not hard to find: it is because we lack the one thing that would enable us to have control over our own affairs — freedom, That was what Andrew Fletcher of Saltoun foresaw in 1707 when the Treaty of Union — that most undemocratic of all agreements — was signed.

The Jacobite cause became a symbol of this lost freedom and that is why it has been subscribed to, romanticised and sentimentalised, particularly in the present day, by people who would have been unlikely to have fought for either the Old or the Young Pretender and who have only the haziest knowledge of history. It is also significant that all those Scots songs about Bonnie

Prince Charlie were written after the event, not like the harrowing Gaelic ones, in the midst of the debacle. Through the Jacobite song tradition, Scottish consciousness became firmly locked into the past. This has been continued with the pre-eminence of Burns's *Scots Wha Hae*, harking back to Bannockburn, as a sort of national anthem, with its rather feebler modern echo in *Flower of Scotland*, the very paradigm of nostalgia. The outdatedness of this backward-looking cult has been admirably counteracted by present day songs such as Hamish Henderson's magnificent *Freedom Come-all-ye* and Brian MacNeill's *No Gods and Precious few Heroes* which pours scorn on the Bonnie Prince Charlie syndrome with lines like

> And tell me will we never hear the end
> O puir bluidy Charlie and Culloden yet again ?
> Tho he ran like a rabbit doon the glen
> And left better folk than him tae be butchered.
> Or are ye sittin in yer cooncil hoose dreamin o yer clan
> Waitin for the Jacobites tae come an free the land ?
> Try goin doun the Broo wi yer claymore in your hand
> And coont aa the princes in the queue!

> There's no gods and precious few heroes
> But plenty on the dole in the land o the leal
> And it's time noo tae sweep the future clear
> O the lies o the past we knew was never real.

Realism and positive forward-looking are healthy signs in present day thinking and this is reflected in the songs. This is the way to encourage Scots to carve out their own destiny rather than dwelling on questionable past glories and lamenting for times that, fortunately, can never return.

If you have doubts that songs can ever influence trends or events, you should listen to some of the political songs that were sung in the sixties and look at what has happened to some of the things they were satirising or protesting against. Scotland has a long history of political satire going back to medieval times, so it was not surprising that two main waves of such songs were triggered by two events of the time: the incorrect and ill-advised adoption of the 'EIIR' logo by the new Queen and the siting of the American Polaris submarines on the Firth of Clyde. Radical elements in Scotland were outraged and there sprang up a crop of anti-royalist, republican songs against the one and anti-nuclear protest songs against the other. Ridicule was the weapon used and a deadly weapon it was.

> Auld Scotland hasnae got a king
> And she hasnae got a queen,
> Hoo can there be a second Liz
> When the first yin's niver been?
>
> CHORUS
> Nae Liz the twa, nae Lilibet the wan,
> Nae Liz will ever dae,
> And we'll mak oor land republican
> In the Scottish breakaway.
>
> Her man's cried the Duke o Edinburgh,
> He's wan o thae kilted Greeks,
> But dinnae blaw his kilt awa,
> For it's Lizzie wears the breeks.
>
> Noo her sister Meg's got a bonnie pair o legs
> But she didnae want a German or a Greek,
> Peter Townsend wis her choice but he didnae please the boys
> So they selt him up the creek.
>
> Sae here's tae the lion the bonnie rampant lion
> And a lang streitch o his paw,
> Gie a Hampden roar and oot the door,
> Ta-ta tae Charlie's maw.

The irreverent and down to earth language of this caused a sensation at the time, but when you think of the recent treatment of royalty by the tabloid press — which was prompted neither by political idealism or moral outrage, but by journalistic desire to exploit the situation — Thurso Berwick aka Morris Blythman does not appear to have exercised his wit too virulently.

The removal of the Stone of Destiny from Westminster Abbey in 1950 had also inspired a number of satirical songs, like *The Wee Magic Stane* which expresses the glee of thousands of Scots at this daring patriotic gesture:

> If ever ye come on a stane wi a ring
> Just sit yersel doun an proclaim yersel king,
> For there'll be nane aroon fur tae challenge your claim
> That ye've crooned yersel king on the Destiny Stane.

The question of whether the one that was returned was the same one that had been removed, revived the whole question of whether Edward I had ever got the right one in the first place. Many people believe it's buried above the village near Dunsinane Hill, as it's unlikely that the Abbot of Scone, a very important man in those days, would have allowed so precious and symbolic a relic to be carried off. What came back to Scotland was a lump of Perthshire sandstone. The whole episode was rich in all kinds of irony and gave a heize to nationalism, in that it revealed far more support for Scottish Home Rule than had been envisaged before.

To turn now to the Campaign for Nuclear Disarmament, to whose banner a strong contingent of Scottish young people flocked, we find the devastating force of Glasgow humour being directed against the politicians and Polaris on the Clyde, using new words to old tunes or parodying older songs:

> Doon at Ardnadam, sittin on the pier
> Alang cam a polis sayin 'Ye'll no sit here!'
> 'Ah but A wull sit here!' 'No but ye'll no sit here!'
> 'Ah but A wull!' 'Naw but ye'll no!' 'Ah but A wull sit here!'

The identification of America with the militarism that many young people saw, and probably justifiably, as a threat to the whole world, led to sit-downs on the pier at Ardnadam and songs like this

O ye cannae spend a dollar when ye're deid,
O ye cannae spend a dollar when ye're deid,
Singin ding-dong dollar, everybody holler,
Ye cannae spend a dollar when ye're deid.

O we'll blaw the yahoo Yankees oot the Clyde,
O we'll blaw the yahoo Yankees oot the Clyde,
Get yer twa-twa-zero an pick them aff the pier O
We'll blaw the yahoo Yankees oot the Clyde.

For we dinnae gie wan hallelujah hoot
If they sail or fly or leave by parachute.
Aa the transatlantic ferries will be fu a Yanks an hairies
An the Clyde will smell the sweeter when they're oot.

These protest songs — which came into being in an era of protest songs like *Blowing in the Wind* — were effective because they were direct and specific, aimed at well-defined and individual targets and not, as so many of the others were, at everything in general but nothing in particular.

In the 1990s, the prestige of the royal family has dwindled as their role has become progressively more controversial. It was quite daring to insult them in the sixties, but now it isn't necessary. The nuclear threat has all but disappeared and has been overtaken by concern with pollution of the environment, the dangers of nuclear dumping and social concerns like unemployment. Did the songs influence the course of events? If it can be said that songs mirror people's concerns, then it must be arguable that they affect what people do and say and the way they treat one another. The wise man quoted by Fletcher was not making an extreme claim, but sagely commenting on what he had observed for himself in the course of time. Certainly it is a fact that many of those who in their young days sang such songs as have been cited, are now to be found among the ranks of those working for social equality, democratic government and humanitarian causes in Scotland. These are, of course, the distinguishing marks of Scottishness, which in the face of the divisive, high-handed and callous dealings of this present government (for which we, the Scottish people, did not vote), continues to struggle and in doing so continues to express its aspirations through the song tradition.

What kind of songs do we find today and who sings them? While it's true, we are still lumbered with the inevitable kilted tenors warbling *Mary of Argyle*, the tartan comics still perpetuating the caricatures of Harry Lauder, the Burns worshippers who can see nothing and no one else before or since the lad from Kyle, we do also have something else. Real Scottish folk music is alive and kicking, even though it seems to be one of the best kept secrets of all time. But there again, if you compare the nineties with the sixties, you can see there have been some changes. Stifled and ignored through the efforts of the establishment to prevent generations of Scots from knowing who they are, the genie is coming out of the bottle, thanks to one or two important uncorking mechanisms that have been at work in the last three decades.

A network of folk clubs has kept up the pressure on public awareness, that there are other kinds of music besides Beethoven or Michael Jackson: every week in many villages, towns and cities, people gather to listen to live music that includes a strong element of traditional or contemporary Scots material. The latest craze among young folk in Glasgow is dancing at ceilidhs. From March to November there is a long series of festivals, in which you can hear unaccompanied ballad singing, bothy songs, fiddling, button accordion, piping and storytelling. Storytelling, which also includes ballad singing, is being taken into schools and the community. New courses in schools demand more Scots language and literature, history and music. John Purser, in his TV series and book, *Scotland's Music*, has made us aware of our magnificent and varied musical heritage, including our folk songs. The Traditional Music and Song Association of Scotland, which runs festivals, ceilidhs and workshops in several parts of the country, is now funded to some degree by the Scottish Arts Council — although they get a pittance compared with Scottish Opera — and perhaps most startling of all, the most successful rock groups in Scotland are those whose material is recognisably Scottish and even political, like Runrig, Hue and Cry, Deacon Blue and the Proclaimers.

As Hamish Henderson discovered years ago when he was helping to found the School of Scottish Studies, the very business of collecting Scots tradition was viewed as a political act. But that hasn't stopped it; on the contrary, it has if anything added impetus. The singers and songwriters of today are no more willing than in the past to deny their roots or keep silent about injustices. The Democracy for Scotland movement has been supported by new songs, the number of which, like the cairn on Calton Hill, is growing.

Folksingers — at least those who earn their living under that label — have always looked on themselves quite rightly as primarily entertainers. Even if you aim to do more than amuse, even if you want people to reflect on your songs, you have first to make sure they enjoy them. But there are singers around in Scotland today who can do both of these things. Two who came to mind are Ian Walker and Nancy Nicolson. Neither of them are ranting, teeth clenching, rabble rousers, but quiet, even gentle performers. It was Ian who used the Selkirk Grace to point the irony of his song about famine in Africa

> From my armchair window on this world, before my eyes appearing,
> Foods for breakfasts, dinners, teas and in between meals feeding.
>
> CHORUS:-
> Some hae meat and canna eat, some wad eat that want it.
> But we hae meat an we can eat, sae let the Lord be thankit.
>
> From my armchair window on this world, I see butter mountains rising,
> And fish thrown back intae the sea, and leaders compromising.
>
> And then I see one bowl of rice, a child's eyes staring at me,
> With feeble bones life never owned, reaching out tae touch me.
>
> Jist doun the road, a million miles, our children they are cryin,
> They canna eat they've got no meat, they spend their livin dyin.

He also makes us look on the unacceptable face of war in which young men are trained 'to search, to find, to kill,' and who look on bombing raids as *The Greatest Thrill:*

 O I was flyin high   (to the tune of *The Shearin's no for You*)
My bonnie bairnie O
I never heard ye cry
My bonnie bairnie O,

I was usin aa ma skill,
Tae search, tae find, tae kill
It wis my life's greatest thrill
Ma bonnie bairnie O.

Nancy Nicolson from Caithness is concerned about the lack of security in nuclear installations like Dounreay and Sellafield and expresses this obliquely but with telling effect in songs like *I'm the Man 'at Muffed It.*

I'm the man 'at muffed it, I'm the man 'at boobed
I'm the man 'at lost the radioactive tube.
I asked ma process workers tae tell ma faur it's geen,
For if it took a dander surely it was seen.

Wullie the crofter, could it be you?
Naw it wisna one I took, I took two.
One 'is peened ma gate shut. the ither 's in ma park,
It's grand fine glow sees me safely through 'e dark.

The fisherman has taken three and the whisky maker four, but they needn't worry, although Caithness may be full of 'plutonium-coated people and radio-active booze' the storeman's lost all his geiger counters too. Nancy's hardest-hitting song is the *Lament for Piper Alpha*, which firmly sites the disaster 'where the graph of the cost crossed the graph of rich pickings tomorrow,' and makes her chorus hammer home the question raised.

Who pays the piper?
Who pays the piper?

Who pays the piper?
Who calls the tune?

Who pays the piper ?
What is the fee?
Flames on the water,
Death on the sea.

I have been among the many others who have made their
contribution to the political song canon when the situation seemed
to call for it. My efforts have included

Hurrah far the weddin o Charlie and Di
We'll aa go tae London in the month o July,
We'll wave our wee flags coloured red white and blue
Three million jobless wi nowt else to do.

There was also one, now out of date, that began, 'Black Maggie,
Black Maggie, the Downing Street bitch,' which I haven't yet
replaced with , 'John Major, John Major the Downing Street dog,'
but it might happen yet. One of my latest political songs was about
democracy and how the government seems to think it quite
appropriate for every other country except this one:

Democracy's for Latvia, Estonia, Lithuania,
Russia, Poland, Germany and even for Albania,
But when we try to claim it, we're told that it's insane we are
It's not for the Scots! Not for the Scots!

Not for the Scots! Not for the Scots!
Why is it good for other folk and not for the Scots?

Like most people I have been appalled and sickened by the war
in Bosnia and one of the worst items of news to be heard in the last
few weeks has been that a mental hospital was having to close down
and send its patients out onto the streets. It makes you wonder
who's really mad:

When the madmen are set free on the streets of Sarajevo
Will they recognise the difference between
The hell that's in their heids an the hell that's aa aroon them
Or will they feel it's only where they've always been?

When their bodies meet the bullets that are fired by their brothers
Will they cry against the injustice an the shame?
Or will they understand as they thole the livin nightmare
Not jist themsels but the world has gone insane?

In the streets of Sarajevo there are wives an mithers mournin
For daith o husbands, slaughter o their sons,
But they won't fear the madmen that wander through the alleys,
They only fear the madmen carrying guns.

One of the most important things that the political song tradition does is keep alive something of the oral tradition, as most of the songs don't appear in books, very few on records and people learn them by hearing them. In this they are like bawdy songs, which is another part of our heritage that expresses our human nature and as such will never die.

Using old tunes to point new words, using parody and humour, using down to earth language — something Fletcher of Saltoun would have understood — these are the stock in trade of the political song writer that have proved effective for generations. Such songs serve their purpose but can hardly be called great poetry or jewels of song tradition. But sometimes a song is crafted by a poet, that marries new words and an old tune into something that expresses our highest aspirations; the result is a song to carry like a banner. I would like to finish with such a song and you can join me, for I'm sure most of you will know it. It is of course Hamish Henderson's incomparable *Freedom Come-all-ye*.

Roch the wind in the clear day's dawin
Blaws the cloods heelster-gowdie owre the bay.
But there's mair nor a roch wind blawin
Thro the great glen o the world the day.

It's a thocht that will gar oor rottans
Aa thae rogues that gang gallus, fresh and gay,
Tak the road and seek ither loanins
For their ill ploys tae sport and play.

Nae mair will the bonnie callants
Mairch tae war when oor braggarts croosely craw,
Nor wee weans fae pitheid and clachan
Murn the ships sailin doun the Broomielaw.
Broken faimlies in lands we've herriet
Will curse Scotland the brave nae mair, nae mair,
Black and white ane til ither mairrit
Mak the vile barracks o their maisters bare.

So come aa ye at hame wi freedom,
Never heed whit the hoodies croak for doom.
In your hoose aa the bairns o Adam
Will find breid, barley bree and paintit room.
When McLean meets wi his freens in Springburn
Aa thae roses and geans will turn tae bloom,
And a black boy frae yont Nyanga
Dings the fell gallows o the burghers doun.

1994

Home Rule

John Home Robertson

John Home Robertson served as Labour MP for Berwickshire and East Lothian from 1978 to 1983, and for East Lothian from 1983 to 2001. In 1999 he was elected as the first Member of the Scottish Parliament for East Lothian since the time of Andrew Fletcher. He was the Minister for Fisheries And Forestry in Donald Dewar's Administration, and in 2001 he became Convener of the Holyrood Progress Group, with responsibility for the completion of Scotland's new Parliament Building.

Home Rule

John Home Robertson

I am grateful to the Saltire Society for the invitation to give this address in commemoration of my illustrious predecessor, Andrew Fletcher of Saltoun. East Lothian, or Haddingtonshire, has returned some remarkable Members to the Parliaments of Scotland and the United Kingdom over the centuries — from Andrew Fletcher to John Mackintosh — so I approach this task with appropriate humility.

Incidentally, I take some pride in the fact that not only Fletcher (from East Lothian), but also my Home family predecessors from Berwickshire, were among those who opposed the incorporating union of 1707 to the bitter end. Parcel of rogues maybe, but not among those bought and sold for English gold.

I do recognise that I am addressing a largely nationalist audience which is a new experience. It is a typically Scottish conundrum that the factions that are in favour of radical constitutional reform apply almost all of their energies to attacking each other. So I have plenty of experience of being rude about the nats, but it is a welcome challenge to be able to approach the subject constructively. I will do my best.

Can I start with a welcome to East Saltoun? East Lothian is a very attractive part of Scotland, with dozens of fiercely independent communities including small villages like this one. It might surprise some people to find that a village like Saltoun is represented not only by a Labour MP and MEP, but also by Labour Regional and District councillors. It was not always thus, but the Conservative and Unionist Party has been effectively confronted and defeated in what used to be its rural strongholds. And we are rather proud of what we have been able to achieve for places like East Saltoun in spite of the obstructive power of the Scottish Office in recent years. By building ten houses for sale to local people at a 50% discount which must be passed on to subsequent buyers (an innovative and ingenious formula); and by building ten more houses to rent in collaboration with the local Housing Association, including two with workshops, we have helped to rejuvenate East Saltoun. The village Primary School, which was on a Tory hit-list for closure, is now bursting at the seams, and it even has its own nursery school.

It is surprising what resourceful and innovative local Councils have been able to do for their citizens in the teeth of Thatcherism. There is a distinction between working the system and collaboration, and I will return to that theme.

When I accepted your invitation last year, John Smith was the Leader of the Opposition, working his way towards an increasingly likely General Election victory. Okay you've heard predictions of Labour victories before, but even hardened cynics can see that the tide is inexorably turning against the Conservative and Unionist government.

John Smith was one of Scotland's best,— totally committed to justice, fairness and efficiency, and totally trustworthy. He was incensed by the abuse of power by an increasingly corrupt and malevolent government, and he understood very clearly that we needed radical constitutional reform to prevent such abuses of power in future, to regenerate our democracy, and to establish genuine civil liberties for our people.

He had been through the fundamental arguments before as the Minister responsible for the Scotland Act in 1978, and the bitter experience of the 1980s has obviously crystallised the case for reform. John had a burning personal commitment to the establishment of a Scottish Parliament, and on his election as Leader of the Labour Party he said repeatedly that he viewed this as a matter of 'personal unfinished business'.

John Smith's high principles have made a deep impression throughout the Labour movement, and I am completely confident that Tony Blair has the same priorities.

It is worth dwelling on the contrast between the politics of devolution in the 1970s and the politics of Home Rule today. Even the terminology is different: it was necessary to talk in code in those days, but now we can call a Scottish Parliament a Scottish Parliament. Frankly there were too many people around who were not ready for the idea yet — not only at Westminster and in England. Let's face it, there were problems in Scotland too, as we discovered when the referendum came.

Yes, the scheme had been mauled in Parliament, and the referendum rules were outrageously rigged, but Scotland was offered an opportunity to elect her own Parliament for the first time since 1707, and the result was 33% yes, 30% no, and 37% abstentions. We were carved up, but we made it easy for them.

The Thatcher experience has created an entirely new scenario. There is a growing consensus for radical constitutional reform not only in Scotland but throughout Britain— the only question is how far it should go. There is an irresistible demand for decentralisation and proper democratic control of government, and a lot of us would like to go on to reform the electoral system and much more. Perhaps we should even spare a thought for the monarchy in its present plight.

Indeed, we are now addressing issues which were on the agenda in Andrew Fletcher's time. The Act of Security passed by the Scottish Parliament in 1703 sought safeguards in relation to the Royal prerogative and royal patronage and these things are still with us. Governments can still make Treaties or go to war under the Royal Prerogative; and Scotland's burgeoning Quangocracy is a grotesque manifestation of the Government's powers of patronage.

These matters are back on the top of the national agenda because of the outrageous excesses of Margaret Thatcher's government, and above all because the self-proclaimed Mother of Parliaments let her get away with it. Supine government backbenchers voted through anything that she asked for — even the poll tax. There is a wonderful irony in the fact that the mother of all centralisation has created the circumstances for the end of all centralisation in the British State.

These are no longer just matters of interest to obscure academics, optimistic idealists and opportunistic politicians. There is now broad agreement throughout the UK that the structure of the State needs to be radically overhauled. People no longer believe that the Westminster Parliament is the fount of all democracy or that it is a wonderful defender of our liberties. Parliament has shown,to its eternal shame, that it cannot always be trusted to resist an oppressive government.

So the case has been made for far more effective democratic safeguards and a major transfer of power away from Whitehall. In due course Wales and the English Regions can decide what that means for them, but there is a well-established consensus in Scotland that we need entrenched democratic control over the existing institutions of government in our nation.

There is no need for a referendum on the establishment of a Parliament for Scotland, but the principle of entrenchment would require a referendum on any future proposal to curtail or abolish the Scottish Parliament. This must be a genuine transfer of power — not just the creation of a subordinate agency that can be abolished at the crack of a whip — like the Greater London Council.

The tactical problems which used to make this such a thorny issue have largely been overcome. The new intake of Labour MPs from the North of England, including Tony Blair, genuinely understand Scotland's aspirations and they also see us as natural allies in their efforts to decentralise power and economic advantages in the new European environment. The dog-in-the-manger syndrome is no longer a serious problem.

Even the abominable no man himself, Tam Dalyell, has been so outraged by the imposition of bad legislation on Scotland through the Westminster Parliament that he has acknowledged the case for accountable government and legisation in Scotland. The West Lothian Question has been turned on its head by experience of the MPs for Westmorland and Westminster voting through oppressive measures which apply to Armadale but not Appleby and to Bathgate but not Bayswater.

There will, perhaps surprisingly, be tactical advantages for an incoming Labour government to introduce legislation to transfer power to Scotland at the earliest opportunity,— because it will substantially reduce the competition for parliamentary time in subsequent Sessions. A new government with a heavy legislative programme would do itself a favour by transferring responsibility for Scottish legislation and scrutiny to Edinburgh as soon as possible. So an early Scotland Bill would be very sound tactics for a new Labour Government's whips and business managers.

And besides, English MPs do not noticeably cherish their right (or whipped obligation) to stay in the House of Commons until all hours of night to vote on Scottish business. So a Scottish Home Rule Bill might be surprisingly popular, although some of the neanderthal Brits who made their name during the Maastricht debate would make a fight of it.

Support for Home Rule here in Scotland is stronger and deeper after the Thatcher years. Scots in Grampian, Tayside and the Borders who voted No in 1979 because they still thought that Westminster was more trustworthy than Edinburgh would reach a very different conclusion today. And even the genteel middle classes have been nauseated by the trasparent unfairness and corruption of recent government of Scotland.

So it is no longer a matter of whether or when Scotland will achieve Home Rule —the only question is precisely how. Is Scotland going to try to storm out of the Union, or are we going to achieve a new settlement by mutual consent? That is the fundamental distinction between the SNP position and that of the Labour Party.

And that takes us right back to the debates preceding the Treaty of Union of 1707 — an independent Scotland, a Union that accommodated the interests of both nations, or the incorporating Union that was imposed in the Treaty. In fact, genuine independence had been lost when James VI took his absolute powers with him to London, so even then the real question was 'what sort of Union?'

Andrew Fletcher was no separatist, as he explained in his pamphlet on the *Controversy Betwixt United and Separate Parliaments* in

1706. He wrote 'It is certainly in the interests of all good men to promote a nearer Union with our neighbours of England; and no time ought to be lost on our part part in going about so good a work'.

I have been re-reading John Mackintosh's thoughts on this aspect of the Home Rule debate. He passionately asserted that he was Scottish and British, and he was an enthusiast for the development of a European identity too. He argued perfectly logically for the positive development of our 'dual nationality'. The fact that we would all fail Norman Tebbit's notorious 'cricket test' with flying colours is not incompatible with our status as Scottish citizens of the United Kingdom.

Both Fletcher and Mackintosh argued that Scotland should have a Parliament to control the government of Scotland, and that it is positively desirable that we should share our sovereignty with our neighbours in certain key areas.

There is no contradiction in that position, it made sense in 1707 and it makes even more sense as we approach the millennium.

It has been amusing to listen to English MPs agonising over the prospect of sharing some aspects of their national sovereignty with our mainland European neighbours three hundred years after the establishment of the British Union. They have a lot to learn.

But of course Andrew Fletcher went on to warn against the dangerous folly of an incorporating Union which would submerge the consideration of Scottish interests in a British Parliament; Fletcher predicted that 'This will be the issue of that darling Plea, of being one and not two; it will be turned upon the Scots with a vengeance; and their 45 Scots Members may dance round to all Eternity, in this trap of their own making'.

I recognise that description all too well, having done my share of dancing around in the trap for fifteen years (including an eternity on the Scottish Local Government Bill Committee). Throughout that period, an overwhelming majority of Scotland's 72 MPs have been committed to Scottish Home Rule, but with the majority in a sovereign Parliament opposed to us we have been held fast in that trap. It has been bad enough for the MPs, but it has been infinitely worse for our long-suffering constituents.

Some of us made the case on various occasions for coordinated action to undermine the authority of the minority administration in the Scottish Office and to challenge its right to impose alien policies. But political gestures can only have limited effects on the conduct of government power endorsed by an elected Parliament.

It would have been irresponsible and wrong to try to incite more active obstruction, firstly because people would have been hurt and secondly because Scots would not have supported it.

We are above all a law-abiding and pragmatic people who try to make the best of difficult situations. Non-payment of the poll tax probably did more harm than good and I am convinced that local authorities like East Lothian have been right to keep using their considerable ingenuity to make the best of a difficult job for our people.

The one major initiative which might have shaken the resolve of the Tory Government on Scotland is the Scottish constitutional Convention. I personally felt that history could have been taking a fresh turn in March 1989 when 55MPs, 59 Local Authorities and representatives from a wide range of Scottish interests met in Edinburgh to sign the Claim of Right.

But the Convention was very seriously weakened by the SNP boycott. That was disappointing, and it may well have delayed progress towards Home Rule. I did note with particular interest that my SNP opponent in this constituency at the 1978 by-election played a prominent part the work of the Convention, and I am even happier to see that Isobel Lindsay is now joining the Labour Party.

There is no straightforward way of altering the sovereignty of the United Kingdom Parliament as long as it continues to resist such reform. Even in the unlikely event of Scotland returning a majority of SNP MPs, it would still be up to that Parliament to decide whether to alter Scotland's constitutional position.

Such a confrontation would be fraught with dangers, and it would certainly not be the smoothest route towards Home Rule.

The recent break-up of the Soviet and Yugoslav federations show just how badly things can go wrong — there is no such thing as a painless divorce.

I find the 'independence or nothing' school of thought in the SNP both depressing and alarming. As I have argued, I think that failure to cooperate with Home Rulers in other parties may have prolonged the life of the incorporating Union. And far more seriously, I think I can recognise some ugly signs of intolerance and even racism in some strands of the Scottish nationalist movement. Could this be part of the pattern of intolerant and intolerable nationalism that is festering in various parts of Europe today? Michael Ignatieff thinks so, and he is well qualified to comment.

I know at least one case where an English family living in this constituency have found 'settler Watch' slogans daubed on their house. And when I joined the thousands of people on the march for Scottish Democracy in Edinburgh in December 1992 I felt very uncomfortable to find myself close to a stamping cohort of nationalists who looked and sounded as though they belonged in the British National Front.

All sorts of people can be found in and around political campaigns, but responsible parties should be aware of the dangers and be prepared to confront them, as we did with the Militant Tendency. It is becoming increasingly difficult to see nationalism in any part of Europe as a progressive influence today. I may have reason to re-emphasise that point after travelling to Bosnia with an Edinburgh Direct Aid Convoy next week.

And is outright sovereign independence worth the candle for a small nation at this stage in history anyway? Can any European national economy defy the power of the Bundesbank? What is the true extent of the independence, or even influence, of the smaller members of the UnitedNations? Where is the security of sovereign states like Bosnia, Georgia, Nicaragua, Lebanon or Rwanda?

And would Scotland be content to be another Denmark or Ireland? Whether we like it or not, Scots played a prominent part in Britain's imperial era, with Scottish soldiers, merchants and missionaries doing at least their share of colonising the Commonwealth and dominating the Victorian world. We all have cousins scattered around the world to prove it.

Perhaps because of that, we have a well developed awareness of international affairs, and we expect to be involved. So, for example, it is no surprise to find Scottish servicemen in UN forces all over the place. I keep meeting them on my travels with the Commons Defence Select Committee.

We take a pride in that sort of thing, and we were furious when the Government started amalgamating Scottish regiments and running down the Rosyth naval complex. Well, how much could an independent Scotland spend on defence, and what would we get for it? Comparisons with other small nations indicate that we would be left with very little — there would be no Scottish armoured infantry battalions or frigates in future UN operations. and no big ships to be refitted at Rosyth.

In due course a European defence structure is going to evolve, but meanwhile the only credible and effective national armed forces in Europe are those of Britain and France. I think that Scots rightly want to remain in the British defence structure, and I offer that as just one important feature of the UK which should not be jeopardised. There are many more.

I have been exploring the developing case for Home Rule within Britain and Europe, and I make no apology for emphasising the risk of jeopardising those aspects of the UK which are good for Scotland and good for the wider world. The establishment of democratic control over Scottish legislation and Scottish government is a constitutional imperative. It should not have been sacrificed in 1707; we were tantalisingly close to restoring it in 1979: and we are about to get another chance.

The incorporating union will pass into history before its 300th anniversary, because the next government of the UK will have not only a firm political commitment to transfer power back to Edinburgh — it will also have a tactical incentive to do so as soon as possible.

There is only one serious risk, and as usual it is homegrown. If we get another display of confusion or division in Scotland, the Unionist extremists will be celebrating all the way to Westminster. We had a glimpse of that sort of mayhem at the Monklands East by-election, where I saw plenty evidence of committed Unionists voting SNP to frustrate Labour's progress towards power and home rule for Scotland. The position of Rupert Murdoch's *Sun* is not as inconsistent as it may seem.

I think that Isobel Lindsay is right to conclude that the Labour Party offers the best prospect of achieving home rule for Scotland, and I hope that a lot more Scottish internationalists like her will help to make absolutely sure that the opportunity is siezed this time. The logic of Andrew Fletcher's case against the incorporating Union is going to prevail at long last, and the election of the new Scottish Parliament will be the most fitting tribute to his memory.

1996

Andrew Fletcher and the Scottish Radical Political Tradition

Edward J Cowan

Ted Cowan lectured at Edinburgh University from 1967 to 1979. He was Professor of History and Chair of Scottish Studies at the University of Guelph, Ontario until 1993 when he became Professor of Scottish History at the University of Glasgow. He is currently Director of the Glasgow-Strathclyde School of Scottish Studies and he chairs the Saltire Society's Committee for the Agnes Mure Mackenzie Scottish History Book of the Year Award. His recent publications include (with Richard Finlay) *Scottish History: The Power of the Past* (2002) and (with Lizanne Henderson) *Scottish Fairy Belief: A History* (2001).

Andrew Fletcher and the Scottish Radical Political Tradition

Edward J Cowan

At the height of the Union dispute in 1703 the Scottish Parliament debated the question of whether to accept the same monarch as England upon the death of Queen Anne. In the event the Scots were to vote an Act of Security accepting the English nomination on certain conditions. In the midst of the discussions Andrew Fletcher of Saltoun put forward a draft act of his own. He presented twelve 'limitations' which should govern Scotland's acceptance of the English royal nominee.[1] The more interesting of the conditions included the following. There should be annual parliaments, the members of which would choose their own president. For every peerage created or granted by the Crown, another county member should be added to parliament. The King should be denied the right to refuse any act passed by the Estates. During the intervals when Parliament was not sitting a Committee appointed by the Estates should administer the government under the King and should be empowered to summon extraordinary sessions of Parliament. Voting by Committee members was to be by ballot. The King was to have no power to declare war or peace, or to agree treaties, without the consent of Parliament. All offices, civil and military, and all pensions, were to be conferred by Parliament. No regiments were to be kept in peace or war except with parliamentary consent. An armed militia of all fencible men between the ages of 16 and 60 was to be maintained. Parliament was to approve all pardons. All law-lords were to be excluded from Parliament or any other public office. Finally, if the King broke any of these conditions the Estates were to declare that he had forfeited his right to the Crown.

To anyone who is the least familiar with the movement towards parliamentary reform in the 18th and 19th centuries, many of Fletcher's ideas will appear strikingly radical or even original. Fletcher was a person who, like ourselves, lived at the end of his century at a moment of profound constitutional and political crisis. He was a man who recognised the economic interdependence of states, a patriot who dreamed of a World Empire, a Scot who looked to the best in his country's past as inspiration for the European and World future. He was disenchanted with self-serving, and cynical, politicians and parties. He was a man who believed that governments encouraged lotteries in order to distract their subjects from the harsh realities which surrounded them. The greatest figures of History speak not just to their contemporaries but to people of all times. Equally when we, posterity, contemplate the past, we cannot escape our own present. The voices of then and now become mixed up — certain statements made three hundred years ago have a particular resonance because of events taking place in the present, which, of course, is why History changes from generation to generation.

If Andrew Fletcher were around in the 1990s instead of the 1690s he would have had an opinion on the developments and events of this week in 1996 — the renewal of the Gulf War, the recovery of Bruce's heart at Melrose, the ever-present problem of homelessness and the long dark shadow of Dunblane. He would doubtless laugh and weep at the beginnings of a parade of English Tory ministers coming north to tell us what is best for Scotland while, on the other side, a shower of shockers, a.k.a. New Labour, cannot even decide how many questions it takes to establish a Scottish Parliament. He would have opinions on the institution of monarchy and the personal inadequacies of certain members of the royal family, on the absence of secure tenancies on the Hebridean island of Eigg, and the crass exploitation of obscure feudal titles. Fletcher would undoubtedly have had something, or much, to say about most of these issues, but though he was a prophet he was not a seer. He was concerned about the universal predicament of humankind. To suggest the contemporary relevance of his views is simply to stress the universality of humanity's predicament.

It is all-too-seldom realised that many of Fletcher's suggestions and concerns arose out of a distinctive Scottish tradition in radical political thinking which long pre-dated his lifetime. We are not here concerned with Fletcher's patriotic ideas during the Union debate, fascinating though these are. Rather it is upon his radicalism, often, admittedly, intimately involved with his patriotism, that we will focus, in examining some of the suggestions he put forward to deal with certain social, economic and political problems in his own day.

Fletcher was described by his old teacher, Gilbert Burnet, as 'a Scotch gentleman of great parts and many virtues, but a most violent republican and extremely passionate', elsewhere toning down his description to 'a most passionate and indiscreet assertor of public liberty'.[2] He was born in 1653 during the Cromwellian occupation of Scotland and he died in 1716 as the Jacobites involved in the Fifteen rebellion were being taken to London for trial. His dying words were allegedly 'my poor country' and throughout an active and controversial career he was passionately devoted to that country, even if, as we now realise, he did not spend all that much time in it.[3]

His early life is obscure though we know he was tutored, from 1664 to 1669, by Gilbert Burnet, later Bishop of Salisbury, before departing on the Grand Tour. Upon his return in 1678 he became M.P. for Haddingtonshire. In the very first session of parliament he attended, he opposed a levy of £30,000 to provide troops for the suppression of covenanters in the south of Scotland. Two years later he attacked the practice of quartering such troops on private citizens. His experience of corruption in Charles II's Scotland and of the ruthless persecution of the covenanters during the 'Killing Times' intensified his revulsion against Stewart despotism. Love them or loathe them, the activities of the later covenanters represent one of the most radical experiments in practical — and perhaps impractical! — politics in European history. Many humble women and men put their lives on the line for their religious and political beliefs and, as a consequence suffered persecution, fines, transportation, imprisonment, state terror and death.[4] It would be of the greatest interest to ascertain exactly how such contemporary developments impacted upon young Fletcher, though we can be pretty certain that they made a profound impression, and we can jalouse that one reaction was the intense disgust which led him to quit Scotland. After a brief flirtation with the Whigs in England he departed for the Continent where he was to be characterised as 'an ingenious but very dangerous fanatic, and doubtless hath some commission for I fear he is very busy and very virulent'.[5]

In 1685 he reluctantly joined Monmouth's rebellion though he was probably fortunate that he did not become entangled in his fellow-countryman Argyll's ill-conceived adventure which would have almost certainly sealed his doom. As it was, his killing of Dare of Taunton alienated some south-western support and so Fletcher personally contributed to the failure of Monmouth's efforts. For his part in the rising he was tried *in absentia* , forfeited, attainted a traitor and sentenced to death. He went into exile in Spain where he collected material for a future pamphlet,[6] the significance of which has generally been underestimated. He also spent a stint engaged upon the respectably millennarian activity of fighting the Turks in Hungary.

He returned to Scotland in the train of William in 1688. At this date he was known as

> a zealous asserter of the liberties of the people and so jealous of the growing power of all Princes in whom he thinks ambition to be natural, that he is not for intrusting the best of them with a power which they can make use of against the people. As he believes all princes made by and for, the good of the people, he is for giving them no power but that of doing good.[7]

For the next fifteen years he was to perform in the main arena of Scottish politics.

Although our knowledge of many of the details of Fletcher's life is deficient, several of his tracts, discourses and speeches have survived. The following discussion concentrates on the *Discourse of Government with relation to Militias* and *Two Discourses concerning the affairs of Scotland*; all three were written in 1698. The other piece to be considered is his *Account of a Conversation concerning a Right Regulation of Governments for the common Good of Mankind* (1703).

The joint themes which run through all of Fletcher's works are those of liberty and resistance to tyranny, which thus place him in the mainstream of Scottish political thought which had been developing since the 14th century. The France of Louis XIV represented for him the essence of the absolutist state closely followed by the example of Stewart England. 'There is not, perhaps, in human affairs, any thing so unaccountable as the indignity and cruelty with which the far greater part of mankind suffer themselves to be used under pretence of government'. He believed that the main aim of government was the enslavement of its citizens; the people were cheated by words and names. If governments retained the ancient terms and outward forms, however much altered, people would 'continue to dream that they still enjoy their former liberty and are not to be wakened till it prove too late'.[8]

One of the instruments of tyranny was the standing army for which reason Fletcher went on to argue in favour of the militia. The citizenry was to be armed: 'arms are the only true badge of liberty'[9]; the militiamen were to elect their own officers and to train, drill and exercise regularly. His ideas would thus appeal to the gun-lobby in a certain powerful country today but Fletcher would have argued that you do not arm *both* a standing army and a militia, not to mention a police force; like many sound democratic ideas this one has been perverted.

Fletcher, however, was convinced that there was nothing so essential to the liberties of the people as placing the sword in the hands of the subject. Freedom evaporated when the sword was transferred — in the form of standing armies — to the hand of the monarch. 'Not only that government is tyrannical which is tyrannically exercised; but all governments are tyrannical, which have not in their constitution, a sufficient security against the arbitrary power of the prince'.[10] He was proud of the fact that the Scots, unlike the English, had never maintained a standing army. Through the militia they had defended their liberty against the Picts, Britons, Romans, Saxons, Danes, Irish, Normans and English, 'as well as against the violence and tyranny of so many of their own princes'.[11] He did have a point here which has rather been forgotten in the welter of tradition which has built up about professional soldiery, about Scottish regiments and fighting Jocks, serving, it should be noted, in the British army. For centuries, though not, perhaps, as far back as the Picts and the Scots whose societies were, in a sense, organised for war, the Scots relied upon *Servitium Scotticanum* or Scottish service to man the national army.[12] From medieval times wappenschaws, or weapon parades, were regularly held. Sports were encouraged in order to keep the citizens fit for military service. Because the Scots had no standing army, and had no foreign enemy save England since the 13th century when they fought off a Norwegian invasion, they consequently had no national debt.

His detailed observations on militias, fascinating though they are, were only part of Fletcher's wider concerns about the tendency of all monarchs towards despotism. He was highly suspicious of all rulers. It was all too often forgotten, in his view, that 'princes were made for the good of nations and not the government of nations framed for private advantages of princes'.[13] There is a famous story, probably apocryphal, that Fletcher mentioned the hereditary Professor of Divinity at Hamburg to a friend who protested that the idea of hereditary professorships was ridiculous. 'Yes!' said Fletcher. 'What think you of an hereditary king?'[14]

Fletcher detected signs of commercial enslavement in the desperate poverty which engulfed Scotland during the last decade of the seventeenth century. He believed that Scottish trade had been systematically suppressed and discriminated against since the Union of the Crowns in 1603. It was for that reason, in part, that he was suspicious of, and opposed to, the proposed parliamentary union of 1707.

The dialogue on *Right Regulation of Governments for the Good of Mankind* is a four-way discussion in which Fletcher plays Devil's Advocate. It was probably founded upon an actual exchange in a London tavern; so far as we know none of the participants seems to have subsequently challenged the factual content of his account. He claimed that English ministers and their sycophantic Scottish counterparts had, since 1603, been concerned to extend English prerogative in Scotland to the ruin of liberty, property and trade; liberty and economic self-determination he regarded as concomitants. He was accused of envisioning improvement in Scotland which belonged in a 'Platonic Commonwealth rather than in the present corruption of things'.[15] He responded by citing the examples of Wales and Ireland neither of which had benefited in the least, economically, through association with England. When it was objected that Ireland was a conquered nation, as was Wales, which thus had no sovereign rights, Fletcher countered, 'I speak of a nation who affirm you have no shadow of right to make laws for them'. England had never shown the least disposition to unite with any other nation throughout its history. 'How your colonies in America are treated is well known to all men'. Elsewhere he had argued that if the Scots established their own constitution in Darien the colony would attract hordes of freedom-seeking Englishmen fleeing the English colonies in America.

All of Europe, he contended, knew of England's hatred of all strangers and inveterate malice towards the Scots. He forced his fellow debaters to agree that the English preference would be to evacuate Ireland entirely and transfer what little trade it enjoyed to London. Wales should be similarly treated as should the six northern counties of England so creating 'a broad ditch to secure you against the Scots'. One of his opponents agreed that if Nature had made such a ditch from the beginning the happiness of England would have been complete. Hadrian's Wall, apparently, did not suffice. He relentlessly forced his argument to the obvious and ironic conclusion that all trade should be concentrated in one place. Essentially his colleagues saw no problems with this proposal and one of them beautifully articulated the attitude of the centre in any country at any period.

> The condition of human affairs necessarily obliges those that govern to attend the good and interest of the whole society and not to be over scrupulous in doing exact justice to particular persons especially if their interest should happen to be different from that of the community. And for this reason, those countries which are most remote from the seat of government ought not to expect an equal participation of liberty and immunities with those that lie at less distance.[16]

Given such a mentality, which daily we are reminded still persists, and prophetic though the above-quoted statements turned out to be, Scotland's outlook appeared extremely poor under the proposed parliamentary and incorporating union which came about in 1707.

Fletcher consistently contrasted the safeguarding of Scottish liberty before the Union of the Crowns with the erosion of that liberty through English absolutism in the course of the seventeenth century. Before 1603, he famously wrote, 'no monarchy in Europe was more limited nor any people more jealous of liberty than the Scots'. There has, however, been a curious failure, even on the part of sympathisers, to see Fletcher in a Scottish context. His debts to the likes of Milton, Harrington, Locke and Machiavelli have often been acknowledged but what has hitherto been missed is that he was very much indebted to, just as he was very much part of, a very important and long-standing Scottish radical political tradition. This is a large and complex subject some of the major aspects of which can only be indicated, rather than explored.

Perhaps the figure of William Wallace provides the neatest and most convenient metaphor for the tradition under review. Rightly or wrongly Wallace came to be seen, over time, as the man from nowhere, the Scottish common man who would come to the fore in his country's hour of need. Furthermore, according to the medieval chronicle tradition, he was betrayed at the Battle of Falkirk (1298) by none other than Robert Bruce. In a fictitious discussion on the banks of the Carron after the battle Bruce questions Wallace as to why he opposes the English king and rejects the advice of the Scottish nobility. Virtually every single Scottish historian, until well into the nineteenth century, wrote of this episode, in which aristocratic opportunism and self-interest, as manifested by Bruce, were contrasted with Wallace's patriotism and native worth, best captured, perhaps, by George Buchanan when he has Wallace address Bruce as follows:

> You to whom ignominious slavery with security is dearer than honourable liberty with danger, embrace the fortune you so much admire. I, in the country which I have so often defended, shall live free, or freely die; nor shall my affection leave me, but with my last breath.[17]

The legend was, of course, much elaborated and popularised by Blind Hary's great poem, *Wallace*, composed, in part, as a kind of anti-English rant in the 1470s. It was one of the first books to be printed in Scotland becoming, indeed, something of a bestseller.

A notable addition to the considerable corpus of myths generated by the Wars of Independence was the Declaration of Arbroath of 1320. In this great document — a letter addressed to the pope by the nobles, barons, freeholders and 'the community of the realm of Scotland' — the Scots enunciated the principle of elective kingship, explicitly discussed their right to remove an unsatisfactory king, and went on to laud freedom as something no-one would ever surrender save with life itself.[18] So angered were some pamphleteers by the failure of the Darien Scheme in the 1690s that they quoted the Arbroath Declaration and Buchanan's version of Wallace's speech. Although the survival and continuity of a resistance tradition from 1320 onwards has been seriously challenged[19] and although there admittedly is no certain evidence that Fletcher had actually read the Arbroath letter, there can be no doubt that he would have sympathised with its contents. It is, however, quite possible that he knew of the document because Gilbert Burnet, made a transcription of a copy of this evocative missive which was kept at nearby Tyninghame, some time during the four years that he was Andrew's tutor at Saltoun.[20]

John Mair believed that kings owed their institution to the people. John Knox forcefully argued that if the king failed to defend religion that obligation devolved upon the people at large. Lindsay of Pitscottie argued that James III was a tyrant who had to be removed in 1488. George Buchanan made a similar case for the deposition of Mary Queen of Scots. He believed that Gaelic Scotland, where chiefs were elected and could be deposed, preserved the customary and time-honoured essentials of the Scottish constitution. There was clearly a contract between a king and his people. In invoking the Celtic past to justify the Scottish present Buchanan appeared to many of his European contemporaries quite strikingly modern:

> So old the tale; but whether merely old
> I leave to each man's judgement. Some may smell
> Mustiness in any thing raked out
> From ancient records; others may call that fresh
> Which matches what is green in memory.[21]

The politically subversive ideas of Buchanan and the concept of parity preached by the presbyterians forced James VI into developing his ideas on Divine Right Kingship or, in other words, absolutism, which ironically ran completely counter to the tradition of Scottish political thinking. The personal union in 1603 allowed him to put some of his ideas into practice. His famous boast, 'Here I sit and govern with my pen; I write and it is done, and by a clerk of the council I govern Scotland which others could not do by the sword', was that of the absolutist. At the time of the Union of the Crowns Sir Thomas Craig anticipated many of Fletcher's arguments on the negative impact of that event. In his tract *De Unione Regnorum Britanniae* Craig wrote:

Towards London the wealth of Scotland will flow . . . Voluntarily and in the friendliest spirit we yield to our neighbours in this union, terms such as they could not have obtained save as the result of the bloodiest war and most conclusive victory.

Interestingly he thought the 'public annals of the two countries should be revised', irritants expunged and a new History of Britain written. When, much later, such a history was manufactured, thousands of Scottish students, in both schools and universities, would suffer the scandalous neglect of their own history while being subjected to an English version of so-called British History, but that was not the fault of Craig. King James was the source of little comfort as he ordered a new flag to be designed and recommended the assimilation of law; 'Scotland subject to English rule must become but as Cumberland and Northumberland and those other remote and northern shires'. He also advocated an incorporating union, an idea which gained no support in either Scotland or England.[22]

At the outbreak of the Covenanting Revolution Alexander Henderson produced his remarkable *Instructions For Defensive Arms* , 1639, which reiterated, as had the the National Covenant the previous year, the idea of the contract between the king and his subjects. He discussed the role of the magistrate, or king, in Calvinist terms:

The people make the magistrate (king) but the magistrate maketh not the people. The people may be without the magistrate but the magistrate cannot be without the people. The body of the magistrate is mortal but the people as a society is immortal.[23]

The constitutional settlement which the covenanters forced on Charles I in 1641 in many respects anticipated Fletcher's limitations upon the Act of Security in 1703. Samuel Rutherford argued at length for the legitimacy of resistance and the elective kingship in his famous *Lex Rex* . In one passage he appeared to question the hereditary principle.[24] A contemporary of Fletcher, Alexander

Shields the covenanter, to take but one example from several radical political theorists who wrote during the 1680s, advocated the contract, the deposition of errant monarchs and a militia along lines very similar to those of 'The Patriot'. In investigating the difference between the king and the tyrant Shields came to the conclusion that there was none; king and tyrant were interchangeable terms, a view which led many of the extreme covenanters to own the republic of Jesus Christ.[25] When James VII fled London in 1688-9 the English claimed he had abdicated; the Scots Parliament stated that he had forfeited his right to the throne. Andrew Fletcher therefore was no voice crying in the wilderness, but was rather the latest in a long line of theorists, not to say extremists, who operated within a very well established Scottish tradition.

Perhaps Fletcher's most radical and most original ideas were articulated when he addressed the twin problems of unemployment and starvation. He wrote during a period of serious famine known as the 'Seven Ill Years'. There were poor harvests in some areas from 1692 onwards but the situation drastically deteriorated between 1695 and 1699 when pernicious weather greatly aggravated the problem. Farms were abandoned, people dropped dead by the wayside. Many contemporary commentators testified to the appalling suffering as the ranks of beggars and the destitute rose alarmingly. The Church announced the nation was being punished for its sins and — in the midst of famine — prescribed fast days.[26]

Fletcher was outraged. Any decent person must feel guilt about 'every delicate morsel' he or she puts in their mouth when they consider the dead and the dying. 'Unnecessary expense in houses and clothes reproach us with our barbarity so long as people born with natural endowment, perhaps not inferior to our own, and fellow citizens perish for want of things absolutely necessary to life'. Famously, his suggested remedy was slavery.

His reasoning was simple. In the Ancient World the master had the obligation to feed, clad and shelter his slaves and their families. There was clearly no such obligation in 1690s Scotland. He attempted to forestall the anticipated outrage of his critics. 'With what face can we oppose the tyranny of princes and recommend such opposition as the highest virtue, if we make ourselves tyrants over the greatest part of mankind?'[27] 'Can any man for whom such a thing has once escaped ever offer to speak for liberty?' He himself was less concerned with names than with things; 'the misapplication of names has confounded everything'. It was said that there was not a single slave in France but, in reality, all French people were slaves to the despotism of Louis XIV. Indeed, the greater part of humankind was enslaved by government. It was Fletcher's recommendation that if, under his proposed scheme, a slave was abused by his master that individual was to be given his freedom and a pension for life. Such advocacy of slavery arose out of his deep-seated humanity. He was not pro-slavery but desperate situations demanded desperate remedies.

The underlying problem in Scotland was the backward state of the country's agriculture. Here again his ideas were self-confessedly visionary. In the first place interest should be abolished thus forcing the wealthy to invest in land. Secondly no man was to possess more land than he could cultivate with the assistance of his employees. In a bid to force capital investment in land he argued that persons working farms which yielded less than £200 per year should convert part of their rents for twenty years purchase. Only those who had incomes of more than £200 per year were to be permitted to purchase such rents, while certain people who were incapable of working the land in person were also to be allowed to buy rents, such as minors, unmarried women and men engaged in public service, for example politicians, soldiers or civil servants. To take a hypothetical example, if rent was £100 a year the farmer would sell half, or £50, to the buyer at twenty years' purchase — that is £50 x 20, which equals £1000. The farmer would then have £1000 to invest in agricultural improvement. Fletcher's scheme would generate prosperity at every level of society and so would boost trade and industry.

His most startling proposal was reserved until last. Teinds and all other dues on the land were to be compounded through cash settlement. But further:

> the tenures of all lands must be made allodial to the end that every
> man be upon an equal foot with another . . . Sure I am that it never
> was nor can be the interest of any prince or commonwealth that
> any subject should in any manner depend upon another subject.[28]

He may have deplored absolute kings but he totally applauded
absolute proprietors. Andrew Fletcher of Saltoun advocated
nothing less than the dismantling of the Scottish feudal system, a
process which, three hundred years later, has still not been
completed.

Fletcher has been described as a friend to his country and to
humankind at the same time. He was a patriot who was also a
citizen of the world and as such, is clearly a person most worthy of,
at the very least, annual celebration, albeit his ideas are still not as
widely known or recognised as they should be. It is, however, very
easy to agree whole-heartedly with Lockhart of Carnwath who
observed that if ever anyone proposed to serve, or merit well of
their country they should think themselves 'sufficiently applauded
and rewarded by obtaining the character of being like Andrew
Fletcher of Saltoun'.

References

1   These are discussed by all of Fletcher's biographers but see W.
     C. Mackenzie, *Andrew Fletcher of Saltoun. His Life and Times*,
     (Edinburgh 1935) 160-84.

2   Mackenzie, *Fletcher*, 1-2.

3   Andrew Fletcher, *Political Works* ed. John Robertson (Cambridge
     1997) xii-xv.

4   Edward J. Cowan 'The Covenanting Tradition in Scottish
     History' in *Scottish History: The Power of the Past* (eds) Edward J
     Cowan and Richard Finlay (Edinburgh 2002) 121-45

5   G. W. T. Omond, *Fletcher of Saltoun* (Edinburgh 1897) 22.

6   John Robertson, 'Andrew Fletcher's Vision of Union' in *Scotland
     and England 1286-1815* ed. Roger A. Mason (Edinburgh 1987) 216-8.

7   Paul Henderson Scott, *Andrew Fletcher and the Treaty of Union*
     (Edinburgh 1992) 4.

8   Fletcher, *Militia* , 3-5. All references are to *The Political Works of
     Andrew Fletcher Esq. of Saltoun* (Glasgow 1749).

9   Fletcher, *Militia* , 35.

10   Fletcher, *Militia*, 7.

11   Fletcher, *Militia*, 46.

12   See Geoffrey Barrow, 'The Army of Alexander III's Scotland' in
     Scotland in the Reign of Alexander III 1249-1286 ed. Norman H. Reid
     (Edinburgh 1990) 132-47.

13   *Account of a Conversation*, 280.

14   Almost everybody who has ever written about Fletcher cites this
     anecdote. Mackenzie, *Fletcher*, 42-3.

15   *Account of a Conversation*, 277.

16   *Account of a Conversation*, 293,299.

17   Edward J. Cowan , 'The Wallace Factor in Scottish History' in
     Images of Scotland eds. Robin Jackson and Sydney Wood *The Journal
     of Scottish Education* Occasional paper No. 1 (Dundee 1987) 5 -18 .

18   Edward J. Cowan, 'Identity, Freedom and the Declaration of
     Arbroath' in *Image and Identity The Making and Re-making of Scotland
     Through the Ages* eds. D. Broun, R. J. Finlay and Michael Lynch
     (Edinburgh 1998) 38-68. See also Edward J. Cowan, *For Freedom
     Alone: The Declaration of Arbroath 1320,* (East Lothian 2002).

19   Roger A. Mason 'Kingship, Tyranny and the Right to resist in Fifteenth-Century Scotland' reprinted in *Kingship and Commonweal Political Thought in Renaissance and Reformation Scotland* (East Linton 1998) 8-35.

20   Sir James Ferguson, *The Declaration of Arbroath* (Edinburgh 1970) 40

21   Edward J. Cowan, 'The political ideas of a covenanting leader: Archibald Campbell, Marquis of Argyll 1607-1661' in *Scots and Britons: Scottish political thought and the union of 1603* ed. Roger A. Mason (Cambridge 19940 241-261. Some of this material is also set out in *Montrose For Covenant and King* (London 1977, Edinburgh 1995) 23-35.

22   Edward J. Cowan, 'The Union of the Crowns and the Crisis of the Constitution in 17th Century Scotland' in *The Satellite State in the 17th and 18th centuries* eds. S.Dyrvik, K.Mykland, J. Oldervoll (Bergen 1979) 121-140.

23   Edward J. Cowan, 'The Making of the National Covenant' in *The Scottish National Covenant in its British Context* ed. John Morrill (Edinburgh 1990) 81 where it is admitted that these noble sentiments are a direct borrowing from Johann Althaus the apologist for the Dutch Revolt.

24   John Coffey, *Politics, Religion and the British Revolutions. The Mind of Samuel Rutherford* (Cambridge 1997) 174.

25   Alexander Shields, *A Hind Let Loose, or an Historical Representation of the Testimonies of the Church of Scotland* (1687) *passim*.

26   William Ferguson, *Scotland 1689 to the Present* (Edinburgh 1968) 78-9.

27   Fletcher , *Second Discourse* , 91.

28   Fletcher, *Second Discourse*, 113-9.

1998

Patriotism as a Passion

Alexander Broadie

Alexander Broadie is Professor of Logic and Rhetoric, at the University of Glasgow. His publications include: *The Tradition of Scottish Philosophy* (1990), *The Scottish Enlightenment: An Anthology* (1997), *Why Scottish Philosophy Matters* (2000), *The Scottish Enlightenment* (2001).

Professor Broadie's lecture 'Patriotism as a Passion' was later included in a slightly extended form in Chapter 4 of *The Scottish Enlightenment*, published by Birlinn in 2001. It is included here by kind permission of the author and the publisher.

Patriotism as a Passion

Alexander Broadie

Patriotism was a common topic in Scotland during the Age of Enlightenment. No doubt part of the reason for this was the fact that Scots had to define their position in relation to Scotland and to Britain. What was the *patria* for patriotic Scots? Was it Scotland or was it Britain? Is it perhaps wrong to think of these alternatives as mutually exclusive? For is it not possible to have patriotic feelings for both Scotland and Britain? The literati, and indeed Scots generally, did not think that these questions were either intellectually or psychologically trivial. I mention them here to give some indication why the topic was on the agenda. It was obvious to the literati that several large questions came in the train of the concept of patriotism. The overarching one asked what patriotism is, and I shall discuss an important answer given by a leading literatus, Lord Kames. In addition patriotism stands in interesting relation to several of the largest ideas that engaged the attention of the literati, in particular the ideas of Enlightenment, of civil liberty and of the commercial stage of society, and I shall explore some of these relations, beginning with the idea of Enlightenment and with the seeming tension between it and patriotism.

The idea of universality has to be to the fore in accounts of the Enlightenment, one reason for this being the fact that the enlightened ones saw themselves as citizens in a Republic of Letters, a Republic which transcends national frontiers, and whose citizens belong to it in virtue of their active participation in discussions and debates conducted in the public arena. We are speaking therefore of people of ideas, men and women of letters, who were, for the purposes of their debates, cosmopolitans, citizens not of Scotland or France or Germany, but of the world. They relied for persuasiveness not at all on a shared nationality but solely on the sheer strength of their arguments. They saw their cosmopolitanism as a virtue, raising them, by means of their intellectual activities, above the particularities and irrational divisiveness of nationalism. Hume declared with pride: 'I am a Citizen of the World.' (*Letters* Oxford 1932, vol.1, p.470) Yet patriotism was regarded as a virtue; to be unpatriotic was a vice that in many eyes would bespeak untrustworthiness, a preparedness even to betray one's country. There is an apparent tension here, for how can patriotism, rooted in the particularity of a country, be a virtue if the cosmopolitanism of the literati, rooted in the universality of reason, is a virtue?

I believe that the short answer to this is that these two sorts of citizenship are not incompatible, but that on the contrary each can support and enrich the other. In effect cosmopolitanism, considered as a moral stance, is respect for certain universal values, those of rationality and of civil liberty. A person who respects these can, without contradiction, also love his country and attach to it a value that he does not ascribe to any other country; a value based upon the fact that the country is *his*. Indeed citizens who embrace cosmopolitanism can only bring benefit to a country. How can a country not be strengthened morally by the presence in it of citizens who attach a high value to rationality and civil liberty?

To take but one example, one of great significance in the eighteenth century, enlightened citizens worked to eradicate slavery. The hostility of the literati to slavery was palpable. It is instructive to realise that some of Adam Smith's most powerful words deal with this issue: 'There is not a negro from the coast of Africa who does not ... possess a degree of magnanimity which the soul of his sordid master is too often scarce capable of conceiving. Fortune never exerted more cruelly her empire over mankind, than when she subjected those nations of heroes to the refuse of the jails of Europe, to wretches who possess the virtues neither of the country which they come from, nor of those which they go to, and whose levity, brutality, and baseness, so justly expose them to the contempt of the vanquished.' (*Theory of Moral Sentiments*, Oxford 1979, pp.206-7) Smith's abolitionist credentials were impeccable. Hume likewise wrote unequivocally against slavery, describing domestic slavery as 'more cruel and oppressive than any civil subjection whatsoever', (*Essays Moral, Political, and Literary*, Indianapolis 1985, p.383) and in that context refers immediately to slavery in the American colonies. And James Dunbar and Gilbert Gerard (son of the more famous Alexander) declared that 'they conceive that the maxims of policy in every well regulated government ought to be consonant to those of morality and consider the slave-trade as equally repugnant to both, as dishonourable to the British name, degrading the Human Nature and diametrically opposite to the genius of the Christian religion.' (King's College Minutes, 3 March 1792) Much the same stand was taken by Francis Hutcheson, Thomas Reid, Adam Ferguson and many others. Civil liberty was demonstrably high on their agenda, and it was a practical, not just a theoretical agenda. In just such ways enlightened ones, through their attachment to a cosmopolitan ideal, could morally enhance the countries in which they lived.

I shall now address the opposite kind of case and consider, not universalism in relation to the particularism of patriotism, but instead the particularism of patriotism in relation to the extreme particularism of *homo economicus*. There seems to be a tension between these two sorts of particularism in the light of Ferguson's discussion of the commercial stage of society and especially of the natural tendency of the commercial life to lead to a fragmented society and to fragmented individuals. It is useful to bear in mind Ferguson's account of the psychopathology of the commercial society: 'It is here, indeed, if ever, that man is sometimes found a detached and a solitary being: he has found an object which sets him in competition with his fellow-creatures, and he deals with them as he does with his cattle and his soil, for the sake of the profits they bring.' (*An Essay on the History of Civil Society*, Cambridge 1995, p.24) In the commercial stage people's self-interest is primary, and the interest that anything else has for us is derived from our self-interest. There is evidently a clash here between the self-love of *homo economicus* and the well-integrated citizen's patriotism, his love of his country. If love of your country is truly *of your country* then it is not just a form of love of yourself. This seemed to Ferguson and to many of his friends to be a real and dangerous problem. The socio-economic form of the problem is: how is commercial life to be squared with civil liberties? It was with this problem in mind that Ferguson called for the introduction of a Scottish militia. Lord Kames, alive to the same problem, suggested a similar solution. I shall turn now to Kames's comments on patriotism and the commercial life. What he has to say is full of interest. He offers a kind of natural history of patriotism and also considers the prospects for patriotism. He is pessimistic, and his pessimism is supported by strong arguments.

As regards patriotism, as with much else, the common Enlightenment view that human history has passed through four stages provides the broad context of discussion; for, given the progress from the hunter-gatherer stage to the pastoral to the agricultural to the commercial, a question arises as to whether or not patriotism is possible at all four stages. The brief answer is 'no'; it is impossible until people have land that they call their own, and that does not happen until the third stage, when people have ceased their wandering and established agricultural settlements. At that point there arises as if by nature a new sentiment or passion, love of one's country for its own sake. This is the passion of patriotism. It can be fitted immediately into a moral framework because it stands in opposition to the vice of self-love, that is, self-love as a governing character trait. To have the vice of self-love is to see every practical question primarily in terms of benefit to the dear self, and if you love your country for its sake and not for your own then self-love, by definition, is not your ruling passion. Kames says of patriotism: 'it triumphs over every selfish motive, and is a firm support to every virtue.' (*Sketches of the History of Man*, Edinburgh 1774, vol.1, p.440) And if he has overstepped the mark in his next comment: 'In fact, wherever it prevails, the morals of the people are found to be pure and correct', there is something to be said for the position. For first, as noted, there is the fact that patriotism is contrary to the spirit of selfishness in which vices naturally take root.

Secondly, Kames sees patriotism as a virtue standing between mutually opposed vices, of despotism on the one side and licentiousness on the other. For despotic rule tends to work against people's love of their country — it is not easy to love a country in which you are oppressed, and not even the despot could easily love a country while most of the citizens are his enemies. Likewise licentiousness, clearly on the side of gross self-indulgence, is about self-love, and when that governs the soul it excludes love of one's country for its own sake. Furthermore each of these opposed vices, of despotism and licentiousness, works against civil liberties. That despotism does so is self-evident. Licentiousness works against civil liberties because licentious acts naturally encroach on other people in all sorts of unwelcome ways, intruding on them and limiting their freedoms. Hence patriotism, by holding these vices at bay, works on the side of civil liberty and virtue.

Patriotism is like all other virtues, in that one cannot afford to relax, smugly, safe in the knowledge that having achieved it one has it for life. Any virtue, and therefore patriotism also, once achieved, has to be maintained. It is always under threat. Kames is clear as regards the chief source of danger: 'Successful commerce is not more advantageous by the wealth and power it immediately bestows, than it is hurtful ultimately by introducing luxury and voluptuousness, which eradicates patriotism.' (*Sketches*, vol.1, p.446) Why it eradicates patriotism is plain: 'No cause hitherto mentioned hath such influence in depressing patriotism, as inequality of rank and riches in an opulent monarchy. A continual influx of wealth into the capital, generates show, luxury, avarice, which are all selfish vices; and selfishness, enslaving the mind, eradicates every fibre of patriotism.' (*Sketches*, vol.1, p.445) The problem for a country is how to achieve commercial success without thereafter being destroyed by it. Kames, as we know, thinks that an education in civic virtue is essential and that that is best achieved through the mechanism of a militia. But he sees no grounds for optimism on this matter. In his *Sketches of the History of Man* he produces numerous examples of countries which, following commercial success gained and for some time maintained by a highly patriotic citizenship, succumbed to riches and luxury, and grew soft and weak. Kames shows how, at least in theory, there can be a cycle here, with a commercially successful country going into decline, and later rising to a renewed success. But he adds: 'The first part of the progress is verified in a thousand instances; but the world has not subsisted long enough to afford any clear instance of the other.' (*Sketches*, vol.1, p.452)

It is in the light of analyses such as these that we should consider Enlightenment ideas about progress and improvement. There have been countless cases of national progress and improvement, but there was a rather common Scottish view, that any such progress requires a holding operation if it is to be maintained, and in the longer run the operation is likely, perhaps even certain, to fail. The literati, all of them educated in Greek and Roman literature, were quick to point to Athens and Rome, which had each had their day in the sun, and did not seem likely to have another such in the foreseeable future. This sad fact does not of course undermine the claim that patriotism is a virtue, but it does tend to support the view that patriotism is one of the more fragile of the virtues. Its value as a bulwark against despotism and licentiousness is not alone sufficient to ensure its preservation.

1999

Scottish Nationality in the Age of Fletcher

Murray Pittock

Murray G. H. Pittock has been Professor in Literature at Strathclyde University since 1996. His recent books include *Inventing and Resisting Britain* (1997), *Jacobitism* (1998), *Celtic Identity and the British Image* (1999) and *Scottish Nationality* (2001).

Scottish Nationality in the Age of Fletcher

Murray Pittock

Nationalism, nationality and national identity are three of the most fashionable areas of intellectual enquiry in literature, history, sociology and politics. This is as it should be, because they are a key dynamic driving the world around us. The title of this paper then seems entirely à *la mode:* but it is not, for one of the central premisses for the study of nationalism is that when Andrew Fletcher of Saltoun was alive it did not exist. Instead, contemporary nationalism theory stresses both the modernity of nationality and its artificiality, triumphantly noting that the first recorded use of 'nationalism' is not until 1836, while tending to occlude the fact that 'nationalist' is found in 1715, 'nationality' in 1691 and 'nation' in 1300. For writers such as Ernest Gellner and Benedict Anderson, whose *Imagined Communities* has been a profoundly influential book, nationalism is primarily a product of the post-1789 era and the new found ability of the literate masses to 'imagine' themselves into a single common identity. Some writers, such as Declan Kiberd, have gone even further in apparently claiming that individual creative artists have 'invented' nationality, as if all that was needed to make a country was an advertising campaign. Other writers speak of 'the narcissism of self-generation' in national narratives.[1] Such terms tell us a lot about our own day, with its instability and plurality of values, its emphasis on choice and illimitable individual possibility and its ironic detachment from all claims to truth not made in a spirit of tolerant provisionality. The issue of prayers in the Scottish Parliament is clearly one with which contemporary theorists of identity would feel at home; but I am going to be asking a different question — how at home would they be with the age of Fletcher? Can they re-enter the past on its own terms, as Sir Herbert Butterfield insisted was always necessary, or are sociologically driven ideas of identity the prisoners of the Whig history they claim to replace, always trying to make the past serve the present?

Perhaps we don't care. But this is not just an academic debate: it is a debate which affects some of the core assumptions about our own country that anybody dedicated to preserving our culture and heritage needs to address. If nations are nineteenth and twentieth-century inventions, then Scotland is just a space in our heads in which we place desires on a par with facts, a place for which the twentieth-century section of the Museum of Scotland, with its stress on personal choices as a substitute for historic achievements, is an apt symbol. If we go down this route, it means that there is no 'authentic' Scottish past or identity to liberate, re-animate, uncover or restore. It means that 'Scotland' is not a metaphysical or even an historic entity, but a place called into being as an expression of contemporary needs. Such a thesis in its extreme form means that Coventry is as Scottish as Scotland is, because there is no 'ish', no quality of the thing in itself separate from what we imagine. Perhaps we should all go down to the West Midlands and imagine hard.

Rather than this, today I am going to re-encounter Fletcher's world on its own terms, and in its own voices. The conclusion will lead us, I believe, to the thesis put forward by the first theorist of nationalism, Ernest Renan, in 1860:

> The nation, even as the individual, is the end product of a long period of work, sacrifice and devotion...our ancestors have made us what we are...To have common glories in the past, a common will in the present; to have accomplished great things together, to wish to do so again, that is the essential condition for being a nation. A nation is a grand solidarity constituted by the sentiment of sacrifices.[2]

Naturally some of these 'sacrifices' and 'solidarities' for us are British ones, for no account of Scotland (or indeed Ireland, though this is often forgotten) today can be purely and solely made in domestically national terms — but this is not so for the age of Fletcher. Before entering it, there is one thing to observe about Renan's definition: it is not an ethnic one. Purely ethno-tribal theories of nationalism are largely straw men articulated by fundamentally anti-nationalist sources: one thinks of the mischievous suggestion that ethnic Scots (whatever those are) living abroad should vote in the 1997 Referendum, a view its proponents would have fled from had it been extended to Irish-Americans.

Ethnicity then can be safely left aside: in Scotland, it was largely made controversial by figures such as John Pinkerton (1758-1826), who were determined to argue in more or less unacceptable ways that 'Scotland has been held back by its degenerate Celtic population'.[3] But long before Pinkerton was born, a mainly Celtic Scottish society had still acknowledged its diversity as a multi-ethnic state, of 'French and English, Scots and Galwegians' as twelfth-century royal charters put it: Norse were later added to the number. It was also a tolerant one: in 1511, the Aberdeen burgh authorities, with commendable sensitivity to the needs of the tourist industry, insisted that the townsfolk release an Englishman from custody because he 'has only come to Town to perform his pilgrimage to St. Ninian', and even radical, with women voting in Inverurie in parish elections as early as 1536, and burgh action against abusive husbands dating back to the seventeenth century. Recent research has suggested that raising the price of alcohol has a tendency to reduce domestic violence: in enlightened Scotland, this was known as early as 1691, when brewers were banned from selling drink to Thomas Rhind, who was guilty of 'stricking and abuseing his owne wyff and familie'. We should not be too complacent, though: one Garioch laird's marginalia stating in sanguinary terms, 'This day oor Jock stickit Glaister o' Glack's auldest son, /Glory be to God the Father, God the Son and God the Holy Ghost'.[4]

Scotland's past was known, respected and used by those who spoke and acted against Union (supporters by contrast, such as Dr

John Arbuthnot, stressed the future and opportunity). Among opponents in the West, some parishes stressed 'the inconsistency of the Union' with the Covenants, and everywhere the addresses, often produced not merely by well-to-do heritors but by more ordinary literate Scots, spoke of the Union as 'destructive to the true interest of the nation'— that 'n' word again.[5] The 'grand solidarity' arising from a long period of common experience was widely articulated, not just in the frequent use of the Declaration of Arbroath as a moniker of Scottish independence (for example in James Anderson's *Scotland Independent* (1705), but also in the speeches of those like Lord Belhaven, with his famous appeal to 'our Ancient Mother Caledonia', in a speech versified as 'We, for a little shining clay, /A kingdom sold'.[6] Although Belhaven had been involved in the 1697 negotiations with the Jacobite court to have Prince James brought up as an Anglican, neither he nor Fletcher (notwithstanding the latter's imprisonment in 1708 on suspicion) can be linked with Jacobite activity, despite Lockhart of Carnwath's view that 'his aversion to the... Union was so great [that] in revenge ... he would have sided with the royal family' ('*Scotland's Ruine*', 44). Nonetheless, Fletcher applauded the Jacobite attempt to dissolve the Union by parliamentary means, made in 1713, which came close to success.

Political will and military muscle to end the Union were mainly the preserve of Scottish Jacobites, even though non-Jacobite anti-Union pamphlets (such as *A Discourse of the Necessity and Seasonableness of an unanimous Address for Dissolving the UNION* (1715)) continued to be produced. So closely were Jacobites associated with anti-Unionism by all parties that it was easy for government propaganda to tar all anti-Unionists as Jacobites. There were several reasons for this Jacobite ascendancy. First, there was the extent to which 'union was implicated in the demonology of the restored regime' of Charles II. Secondly, they were the only group with a coherent single main policy; thirdly, they alone were likely to attract major magnate support (17 dukes, marquesses and earls had their names appended to a 1707 call for a restoration); fourthly, their appeal to the Scottish royal line was more convincing to many than Fletcher's quasi-republican politics, and fifthly and sixthly they tended also to be more absolute than he, as well as more sympathetic to the traditional national identity of Scotland, with its Celtic-led iconography. Fletcher by contrast appears to have had some sympathy for the 'shared Gothic inheritance' of Britishness[7].

These conclusions may seem surprising: but although Fletcher was the most astute critic of the Union, correctly pointing out that the concentration of power in London would also lead to a concentration of economic resources, his espousal of a confederal relationship between Scotland and England in a looser monarchical Union arguably marks him out as more of a genuine proto-federalist than those who stressed 'independency', for

> in a state of separation from England, my country would be perpetually involved in bloody and destructive wars. And if we should be united to that kingdom in any other manner [but that of confederal equality], we must of necessity fall under the miserable and languishing condition of all places that depend upon a remote seat of government. (Fletcher, 214).

As a political theorist and a patriot, Fletcher's vision was acute in that it diagnosed the structural limitations of an incorporating union; but his alternatives had limited popular appeal. Born out of abstract reasoning, Fletcher's politics lacked the soundbite draw of 'No Popery, No Hanover, No Union' proclaimed in 1715 at Inverness, or the calls for 'King James the Eight . . . and No Union' at Glenfinnan thirty years later[8]. The appeal to the restored Stuart line was an appeal (as is clear from the underlying ideology of De Wet's 1684-6 Holyrood portraits) to the restoration of history, the freeing of Scotland from the Year Zero of 1688 or even (as James Macmillan has recently reminded us) 1560. It was this appeal to a common lost history which lay underneath many of the patriotic statements of the period, a period whose practices were still far more in accord with Scottish tradition than any British society. For example, to take the case of the law, only one of the professions retained for Scotland by the Union, it remained true that 'as many as 40 per cent of the admissions to the faculty of advocates between 1660 and 1750 had studied in Dutch universities', while 'only two of the 10,917 entrants to the Inns of Court between 1590 and 1639 were Scots' [9].

Scottish traditions were frequently expressed in terms of a struggle for liberty, often performed through military feats, and this was true of anti-Unionist expressions at all levels of society. On 4 November 1706 the Duke of Hamilton spoke on 'consideration of the first article' of Union in these terms:

> Shall we in half an hour yield what our forefathers maintained with their lives and fortunes for many ages ? Are none of the descendants here of those worthy patriots who defended the liberty of their country against all invaders . . .

Sixteen days later, those who conspired to burn the articles at Dumfries wrote from their more humble social rank in the same terms: praising 'the sovereignty of this our native ancient nation . . . purchased and maintained by our ancestors with their blood'. The authors went on to appeal to the 'martial . . . spirits of Scotsmen' not 'to be disposed of at the pleasure of another nation'. These were the means through which Scottish patriotism frequently expressed itself in the age of Fletcher, himself described by Lockhart within the same metaphor as 'as brave as his sword' (*'Scotland's Ruine'*, 43, 160, 177-9). Union was on this reading, like the overthrow of the Stuarts, born out of an act of collective disloyalty to a past of valour and simplicity, an image still alive not only in the pages of Burns but also in the Scottish Renaissance (for example, Edwin Muir's 'We were a tribe, a family, a people')[10]. Scotland, like Rome, had been preserved by the force of her citizen's arms, a view hinted at by figures as disparate as Samuel Johnson and Jonathan Forbes, the Quaker who would not leave the field of Culloden until he had let 'daylicht into three of the English deevils'. Had he had the benefit of modem historical knowledge, Forbes would have known that Jacobitism was a civil war which had nothing to do with nationality, so we must forgive his ignorance, one shared not only by fellow-Jacobites like William Hamilton and John Roy Stewart, but by the British government of his day. Government propaganda showed the Jacobites flying Scottish national emblems, political cartoons such as *The Chevalier's Market* emphasized the link between Jacobitism and anti-Unionism and Lord Chesterfield remarked 'if Scotland be not an enemy country, I don't know what country can ever be called one'[11]. If words were not enough actions spoke louder: not only, as Daniel Szechi has recently discovered, did the government prevent the forming of even pro-Hanoverian Scots militias in 1715, but it was not until 1797 that Scotland was permitted a domestic militia at all (Brown, 247). The link between nationalism and military valour was taken seriously by those who feared it.

In Jacobite circles, the exaltation of the sword as a heroic weapon expressed a warrior history and tradition reaching back to the Scots-Irish warband of the Fianna, and eventually incorporated into the work of James Macpherson. Stories of wonderful deeds with the sword at Culloden abound, and are a mainstay of Gaelic heroic poetry. Jacobitism also celebrated the warrior past of Scotland strongly in more general terms. It was in this vein that James Philp composed his epic on Viscount Dundee, *The Grameid* (a tale of 'glorious deeds and uncontaminated fidelity' (Pittock, 1994, 41), and that Dr Patrick Abercromby, sometime physician to James VII, published his *Martial Achievements of the Scottish Nation* while supporting the Stuart war effort in 1715[12]. Similarly, James VIII himself, in his declaration of December 1743, drew attention to 'a Nation always famous for valour . . . reduced to the Condition of a Province', while in 1718 the Earl of Mar wrote on his King's behalf of breaking 'the unhappy union' by 'force of arms', and thus restoring the 'free and independent' condition of ancient valour [13]. It was to this tradition too that Lord Lovat appealed in his last words from the scaffold, '*Dulce et decorum est pro patria mori*'. When, during the 1822 visit, Sir Walter Scott drew attention to the military valour of Scotland in the wake of the Napoleonic Wars, he knew what he was doing: not inventing the nation, as the sloppy demythologizing readings of our own day suggest, but re-animating the umbilical link between Scottish valour, independency and monarchy which had perished in the anti-Union struggles of the eighteenth century. What was truly illusory in his rendition was not tartan, a patriotic symbol for at least 150 years, but the notion of independency itself: the theatrical appearance of the Honours of Scotland completed Sir Walter's fable, but the *Letters of Malachi Malagrowther* were to bear witness to the reality of sovereign authority. The place where it resided was to be moved not by theatre, but complaint.

Military and physical renewal were often linked, as the idea that the Union represented a kind of voluntary national enfeeblement (note how many of Burns's Jacobite and anti-Union songs are in the mouths of old men, representatives of a defeated nation). In December 1706, an Aberdeen schoolmaster expressed it thus:

> Here lies, entombed in her own ashes, yet with the hope of a blessed resurrection, the famous nation of the Scots . . . she, full of years, though yet in undiminished vigour of limbs, losing control of her mind, yielded helpless to fate. Pray for her! [14]

Similarly, the 'parcel of rogues' who formed 'the awkward squad' are portrayed in that poem as feeding on a weakened Scotland's 'vitals like vultures'. From this position of decline and weakness, only the restoration of the Stuart with its promise, in Iain Mac Lachlainn's words of 'smooth rigs . . . the corn-field now cleansed of its weeds' can renew the country [15]. Elsewhere there are stronger and more direct sentiments, which at times verge on despair. In 'A speech without doors upon the present state of the Nation' (1718) the writer bewails 'the black designs of the english', 'a nation ever intent upon our ruin and destruction', who have, together with their Scots allies, procured 'this master piece of villany they call by the name of an incorporating union' which has 'constrain'd us to depend upon a remote seat of government'. [16]

The strength of these feelings was expressed in the Jacobite Rising of 1715, whose banner bore the legend *Nemo me impune lacessit* beneath the words 'No union', while its hanging pendants bore the words 'for our wronged king and oppressed country' and 'for ourselves and liberties'[17]. Crucially important for any interpretation of nationality is the significant evidence that the Stuart cause was itself to an extent only a motor for anti-Union feeling. This ranges from the intense military mobilization of 1715, four of five times the maximum achieved by the dynastic royalists Dundee and Montrose, to statements such as that made by Mar to Spalding of Ashentullie on offering him a colonel's commission, stating that 'whether James landed or not the intention was to march south, dissolve the Union and redress the grievances of Scotland'. Even in Argyll, Campbell tenants were reported 'in favour of a Scottish rising [no mention of the king, note] against the Union', while an address was printed at Edinburgh calling for an end to 'the late unhappy union'. Mar reverted to the traditional pre-Union Scots taxation system and proposed an Association 'never to admit of Terms till the King was restored, the Union broken and the [Episcopal] Church establisht'; whatever his failings as a general, some one in twelve adult males joined his forces (Pittock, 1998, 41-2). The symbiotic aim to, in Lockhart of Carnwath's words, 'redeem the nation and restore the King', remained a core component of Jacobite policy. Redeeming nations, and restoring their ancient rights and independent state may seem a bit like nationalism, but let's not get carried away. After all, if things are what they seem, what would theorists of nationalism have to interpret?[18]

Although in 1698 Fletcher had remarked that 'the Party of the late King James was always insignificant, and is now become a jest' (Fletcher, 44), the Union which he opposed was to change matters radically. As Lockhart put it:

> people of all ranks and perswasions were more and more chagrined and displeased, and resented the loss of soveraignty, and were daily more and more perswaded that nothing but the restoration of the royal family, and that by the means of Scotsmen, could restore them to their rights...nothing was to be heard throughout all the country

save an universal declaration in favour of the king and exclamations
against the Union and those that had promoted it. ('*Scotland's Ruine*',
210-11).

Even allowing for the exaggeration of a partisan, there is significant
evidence which bears out Lockhart's claims. In the 1710 election, 16
out of 45 seats were taken by Jacobites, including 'Fife, Perthshire,
Dumfriesshire, Forfarshire, Wigton Burghs, Ross-shire, Aberdeenshire,
Inverness Burghs, Lanarkshire, Linlithgowshire and Linlithgow'[19]. In
1715, 261 JPs were dismissed for suspected Jacobitism, but that this
was ineffective is borne witness to by the fact that 'after the rising'
more than 30 per cent (rising to 54 in Forfarshire and 77 per cent in
Kincardineshire) were dismissed in the country between the Moray
Firth and the Tay [20]. Lockhart, one of the two prime movers for repeal
of the Union in 1713 (the other was Lord Balmerino), became, despite
the Whiggish background of his family, King James's main agent in
Scotland. In 1719, we find him pressing the Earl Marischal on the
'heartie aversion to the Union' among Presbyterians . At the time of
the Malt Tax riots in 1725, he wrote to the King in exile to tell him
exactly what was needed: 'as the aversion to the Union dayly encreases,
that is the handle by which Scotsmen will be raised to make a general
and zealous appearance'. James was not behindhand in seeing the
policy significance of such appeals, nor was his son: as late as
November 1746, Charles wrote in a memo to Louis XV that the
kingdom of Scotland was 'about to be destroyed' by 'the English
government'. Such an appeal was designed to gain a sympathetic
hearing from the decision makers of France, whose repeated efforts
to divide Britain into its component states in the eighteenth century
formed a major feature of Bourbon and indeed Directory foreign
policy seldom recorded in mainstream British history. In 1708, 1745,
1759 and 1798 French military plans were aimed at this goal, and
in the late 1740s the Marquis d'Eguilles prepared a memorandum
on options for a future Scottish government which included the
serious plan to establish a republic in Scotland': would Fletcher
have approved? (Pittock, 1995, 88-95).

Historically, one can argue that such moves, while crucial in France's struggle to prevail as foremost world power, also drew on the symbiosis between France and Scotland briefly achieved in the regnal union of 1558-60. Material to this effect is certainly found in Scotland, for example in one of the earliest versions of 'Auld Lang Syne' which, interestingly, recommends not British, but Scoto-French union, in memory of 1558-60: 'Why did you thy Union break! thou had of late with *France*' it complains [21]. It is interesting to think that Burns's world-famous song may have its roots not only in a Jacobite set (as 'A Man's a Man' does) but also in one which recommends Scoto-French Union. That these were not isolated sentiments is suggested by Daniel Defoe's satirizing potential Scoto-French union in *The Advantages of the Act of Security* (1706). Songs circulated widely in Scotland both as a means of expressing political solidarity (remembering Fletcher's famous statement about their being more important than laws), and also in tandem with military activity and other forms of the popular display of discontent. Anti-Union songs were common in Scots and English, and are also found in Gaelic, such as Iain Lom's 'Song Against the Union', while appeals to 'Scotland's honour' and 'warlike Scota' are found widely in a Gaelic poetry which fears the fate of being 'thralls beneath the English'[22]. They expressed the desire to 'o'erturn' the 'union' 'which caus'd our nation mourn' (Pittock, 1994, 138). Occasionally linguistic nationalism is evident. In 'Lochmaben Gate', written to commemorate a 1714 wapenschaw in the southwest, the travelling speaker encounters a Whig who talks to him in perfect English: 'These are rebels to the throne, / Reason have we all to know it; / Popish knaves and dogs each one'. The speaker 'ettled' while his 'heart was like to scunner' and answers in Scots, 'Deil send a' the whiggish race / Downward to the dad that gat 'em' ('dad' being a friendly term used of a ruler dating back at least to the 1590s). This association of Scots language with the 'true' and 'traditional' nation can also be found in the arguments of sixteenth-century Catholic apologists like Ninian Winzet: there were some Jacobites as late as 1745 who liked to keep alive the speech of Court Scots, and it was common among exiled Jacobites to take 'considerable pleasure in things Scottish, from the country's history to its tastes and mores'[23]. Songs such as 'The Broad Swords of Scotland' likewise harked back to the great theme of Scottish valour, mourning that 'we're all sold' who once were 'valiant and bold': Burns of course makes a similar point in 'Parcel of Rogues'. 'The Curses' is even stronger:

> Curs'd be those traitorous traitors who,
>   By their perfidious knavery,
> Have brought our nation now into
>   An everlasting slavery.
> Curs'd be the parliament, that day,
>   Who gave the confirmation;
> And curs'd be every whining Whig,
>   And damn'd be the whole nation.[24]

While a sense of utter despair is found here and in other songs, there is also the hope of renewal, that 'Scotland rejoice, from Bondage you're free, / You're a Nation again, and ever shall be' (Pittock, 1994, 163).

Sentiments of these kinds were unsurprisingly expressed anonymously; but writers like Allan Ramsay could make the same points: in the vision of the underworld in his elegy on Archibald Pitcairne, traitors float on 'a pool of boiling gold' reserved for 'those who their country sold', and then more explicitly 'he the faces of some traitors knew / Who at the U(nion) did their hands embrew, / In the heart blood of ancient Caledon'. Ramsay's Easy Club of course addressed George I in 1715 calling for a repeal of the Union, while in 'The Vision', Ramsay revisits the Wars of Independence to provide a language for contemporary politics (Pittock , 1994, 154-7). Sometimes life (and death) itself echoed into legend through poetry. The account of Lord Balmerino's execution in 1746 puts it thus: 'brave Balmerrony . . . in the midst of all his foes /Claps Tartan on his eyes ... A Scots Man I livd ... A Scots Man now I die . . . May all the Scots my footsteps trace'. [25] Literature with this kind of outlook both expressed the aims of the Jacobite leadership and was subscribed to by them: in 1745, Oliphant of Gask, along with other Jacobite leaders, was asked to subscribe 'for a new edition of Fordun's Scotichronicon'. Gask's son Laurence was, with Lord Ogilvie the titular Earl of Airlie, among 'the last partisans of the alliance between France and Scotland', which derived from the patriotism of that era.[26]

These are the views of those who stated their support for Scottish nationality in the age of Fletcher. There were, of course, many who did not share these views: who, even if they resented the events of 1707, appreciated their opportunities, or whose religious outlook prevailed over any issues of national difference.

But for those who spoke of nationality in these terms, I am going to premiss the word 'nationalist', fortuitously first recorded at the time of the Rising of 1715. There are those who will assuredly disagree, but William of Occam, who probably died in the Black Death in 1349, famously warned us against multiplying entities beyond necessity under the terms of that intellectual principle known as 'Occam's Razor'. In other words, if it looks like a dog, smells like a dog and barks like a dog, it's a dog. With that in mind I conclude with the words of Professor James Garden, preached from the pulpit in Aberdeen in 1715:

> . . . the wealth and strength of this nation has been exhausted and our land in a great measure dispeopled: with the loss of the Liberty, privileges and independency of this our Ancient Kingdom . . . the Nation basely and shamefully . . . sold and enslaved...under the specious name and pretence of an Union with England.[27]

All these words: nation, liberty, independency are echoes from the age of Fletcher, not a foreign tongue from a world before nationalism existed.

References

1 John Hutchinson and Anthony D. Smith, *Nationalism*, (Oxford and New York: Oxford University Press, 1994), 89-96, 178,306,317.
2 Ernest Renan, 'Qu'est-ce qu'une nation?' in ibid, 17-18.
3 William Ferguson, *The Identity of the Scottish Nation*, (Edinburgh: Edinburgh University Press, 1998), 253.
4 'An Alphabetical Index of the first 67 volumes of the Council Register'(Kennedy Index: Council Register 41), Burgess Regulations 1632-94, p. 27, Aberdeen City Archives; *Records of Old Aberdeen*, ed. Alexander MacDonald Munro, New Spalding Club, 2 vols, (1899,1909), 1:155; W. Douglas Simpson, *The Earldom of Mar*, (Aberdeen, 1959), 106, 145; A.A.M Duncan, *Scotland: The Making of the Kingdom*, (Edinburgh: Oliver and Boyd, 1978 (1975)), 126, 141.
5 *'Scotland's Ruine': Lockhart of Carnwath's Memoirs of the Union*, ed. Daniel Szechi with a foreword by Paul Scott, (Aberdeen: Assocation for Scottish Literary Studies, 1995), 148-9.
6 Murray G.H. Pittock, *Poetry and Jacobite Politics in Eighteenth-Century Britain and Ireland*, (Cambridge: Cambridge University Press,1994), 6, 153.
7 Colin Kidd, 'Protestantism, constitutionalism and British identity under the later Stuarts' in Brendan Bradshaw and Peter Roberts (eds), *British consciousness and identity*, (Cambridge: Cambridge University Press, 1998), 321-42(323,341).
8 Andrew Fletcher, *Political Works*, ed. John Robertson, (Cambridge: Cambridge University Press, 1997), 214; Michael Hook and Walter Ross, *The 'Forty-Five*, (Edinburgh: HMSO, 1995), 26. I am also indebted to Daniel Szechi's research here, which is forthcoming in his Yale study of the 'Fifteen.
9 Keith Brown, 'Scottish identity in the seventeenth century' in Bradshaw and Roberts (1998), 236-58 (241).
10 From 'Scotland 1941'.
11 Murray G.H. Pittock, *Jacobitism*, (Basingstoke: Macmillan, 1998), 112.

12   Alistair and Henrietta Tayler, *Jacobites of Aberdeenshire and Banffshire in the Forty-Five,* (Aberdeen, 1928), 186; *Jacobites of Aberdeenshire and Banffs hire in the Rising of 1715,* (Edinburgh and London,1934).

13   Murray G.H. Pittock, *The Myth of the Jacobite Clans,* (Edinburgh: Edinburgh University Press, 1995), 92,96.

14   Agnes Mure Mackenzie, *Scottish Pageant 1707-1802,* (Edinburgh, 1950), 329.

15   G.S. Macquoid, *Jacobite Songs and Ballads,* (London: Walter Scott, n.d.), 51; John Lorne Campbell, *Highland Songs of the Forty-Five,* (Edinburgh: John Grant, 1933), 5.

16   National Library of Scotland MS 6290 f. 145.

17   Alistair and Henrietta Tayler, *1715: The Story of the Rising,* (London and Edinburgh, 1936), 36-7,41.

18   *Letters* of *George Lockhart of Carnwath,* ed. Daniel Szechi, (Edinburgh: Scottish History Society, 1989), 141.

19   Daniel Szechi, *Jacobitism and Tory Politics, 1710-14,* (Edinburgh: John Donald, 1984), 67; *Letters of George Lockhart,* 5n, 53n, 58n, 75n, 76n, 85n, 95n.

20   Michael Lynch, *Scotland: A New History,* (London: Century, 1991), 327.

21   NLS Rosebery 117.

22   Lorne Campbell (1933), 31, 119, 129.

23   Daniel Szechi, 'Came Ye O'er Frae France?: Exile and the Mind of Scottish Jacobitism, 1716-1727', *Journal of British Studies* 37:4(1998), 357-90 (375).

24   James Hogg, *The Jacobite Relics of Scotland,* (Paisley: Alex. Gardner, 1874), 78-9, 105, 133.

25   Aberdeen University Library MS 2222, printed in Murray Pittock, 'New Jacobite Songs of the 'Forty-five', *Studies in Voltaire and the Eighteenth Century* 267(1989), 1-75.

26   T.L. Kingston Oliphant, *The Jacobite Lairds of Gask,* The Grampian Club, (London: Charles Griffin and Co., 1870), 102,428.

27   NLS MS 1012.

About the Saltire Society

The Saltire Society was founded in 1936 at a time when many of the distinctive features of Scotland and its culture seemed in jeopardy. Over the years its members, who have included many of Scotland's most distinguished scholars and creative artists, have fought to preserve and present the nation's cultural heritage so that Scotland might once again be a creative force in European civilisation. As well as publishing books and producing recordings the Society makes a number of national awards for excellence in fields as diverse as housing design, civil engineering, historical publication and scientific research. There are Saltire Society branches in many towns and cities in Scotland and beyond, and each year members organise dozens of lectures, seminars and conferences on important aspects of Scottish culture.

The Society has no political affiliation and welcomes as members all who share its aims. Further information from The Administrator, The Saltire Society, Fountain Close, 22 High Street. Edinburgh, EH1 ITF Telephone 0131 556 1836.

Alternatively, you can make contact by email at saltire@saltire.org.uk. and visit the Society web site at www.saltire-society.demon.co.uk